HUMAN DEVELOPMENT AND HUMAN POSSIBILITY

Erikson in the Light of Heidegger

Richard T. Knowles

UNIVERSITY
PRESS OF
AMERICA

LANHAM • NEW YORK • LONDON

Copyright © 1986 by

University Press of America,® Inc.

4720 Boston Way
Lanham, MD 20706

Library of Congress Cataloging in Publication Data

Knowles, Richard T., 1934-

   Human development and human possibility.

   Bibliography: p.
   Includes index.
   1. Developmental psychology.   2. Philosophical
anthropology—History—20th century.   3. Erikson,
Erik H. (Erik Homburger), 1902-   .   4. Heidegger
Martin, 1889-1976.   I. Title.
BF713.K58   1985   155.4   85-20498
ISBN 0-8191-4992-6 (alk. paper)
ISBN 0-8191-4993-4 (pbk. : alk. paper)

All University Press of America books are produced on acid-free
paper which exceeds the minimum standards set by the National
Historical Publications and Records Commission.

To my mother and

to my wife, Tracey

ACKNOWLEDGEMENTS

Without the existence and support of the Psychology Department of Duquesne University I would not have had the courage to state these ideas, much less to spell out their implications. Accordingly, I am grateful to Adrian van Kaam for founding the department and to Amedeo Giorgi for carrying forward the vision of psychology as a human science as represented by the department. The encouragement of my friend and colleague, Charles Maes, has been an important background factor for my work in the department. David Smith, another friend and colleague, has also given his support as have my other colleagues, Anthony Barton, Constance Fischer, William Fischer, Edward Murray, Paul Richer and Rolf von Eckartsberg. I also want to thank the hundreds of Duquesne graduate students who have attended this course. A very special group of dedicated students, they have taught me much. The final impetus for the book came from the encouragement of my wife, Tracey. She supported this work not only in words but in actions; for, it was she who typed and corrected the previous drafts of this book. For her love, encouragement and help, I am deeply grateful.

CONTENTS

ix

LIST OF FIGURES

PREFACE

This text is intended primarily for a developmental psychology course for practitioners, especially at the graduate level. It has been used successfully for ten years in a Masters degree program for those intending to go on to become clinical psychologists. Because of its therapeutic orientation it would seem especially appropriate for Masters degree courses in such applied fields as social work, pastoral counseling, school psychology, counseling psychology, guidance and counseling and so on.

This text could also be used in undergraduate courses in developmental psychology in which a more integrated, humanistic approach is desired. In such courses it could serve as the main text. For the more traditional courses in developmental psychology it might be used as a secondary one in order to bring out certain contrasts.

What distinguishes this book from others in the field is that it belongs to a different stream of thought. It strives to carry on a tradition represented by such authors as Ludwig Binswanger and Medard Boss, two European psychiatrists who found in Heidegger's work a corrective to psychoanalysis. This text attempts to be a further extension of their work in phenomenological psychology.

In this country that tradition is carried on by the Psychology Department of Duquesne University. The project of the Department is to refound the science of psychology as a human science rather than to carry on the natural scientific orientation to psychology. This is a text which applies this project to the area of human development. It makes use of the contributions of phenomenologically oriented philosophers and psychologists in attempting to understand developmental psychology from a human scientific point of view.

Only an entity which, in its Being, is essentially futural so that it is free for its death and can let itself be thrown back upon its factical "there" by shattering itself against death - that is to say, only an entity which, as futural, is equiprimordially in the process of having-been, can, by handing down to itself the possibility it has inherited, take over its own thrownness and be in the moment of vision for 'its time'.

Authentic Being-one's-Self does not rest upon an exceptional condition of the subject, a condition that has been detached from the "they"; it is rather an existentiell modification of the "they". . .

Along with the sober anxiety which brings us face to face with our individualized potentiality-for-Being, there goes an unshakable joy in this possibility.

- Heidegger, Being and Time

CHAPTER ONE

THE CARE STRUCTURE AS THE GENERAL FRAMEWORK

FOR UNDERSTANDING ERIKSON'S

THEORY OF DEVELOPMENT

This chapter is meant to be illustrative of the general framework which will be used throughout the book; it is not meant to be immediately convincing since the final appeal is to experience rather than to theoretical niceties. However, it does seem to me that the theoretical statements made here, despite their conclusive tone, reflect experience and provide a broader and more integrated way of understanding human development. This chapter could have come at the end of the book after a piece-by-piece case had been made for each of the statements in the other chapters. However, I think it is more helpful to the reader to present the integrating framework at the beginning and to show the unfolding of the framework in the following chapters.

The general framework outlined here is a way of understanding Erik Erikson's developmental contributions within a broader paradigm, that of the Care Structure, the central structure of existence according to Martin Heidegger (1927/1962, p. 237). Erikson's developmental theory is accepted and his terminology is used throughout. The contention here is that Erikson's theory, as valuable as it presently is, would be even more valuable if broadened beyond the psychoanalytic paradigm within which it rests. The psychoanalytic paradigm is affirmed but only as a partial perspective; the attempt here is to broaden Erikson's perspective in much the same way as he has broadened the traditional psychoanalytic perspective. However, in this case, the broadening is to extend beyond the limits of psychoanalysis and to include experiences and concepts ordinarily excluded from it. The attempt is to overcome the narrowness of a particular specialized appoach without resorting to a "sloppy eclecticism." The attempt is to broaden and to arrive at an integration of developmental concepts which may hold more promise than either a single specialized approach or a group of disconnected specialized approaches, the two alternatives currently available.

Erikson's Three-Pronged Approach

The work of Erikson lends itself to such an integration better than the more orthodox forms of psychoanalysis because he has already broadened in a careful way the focus of psychoanalysis. He has been guided by Freud's original developmental emphases (oral, anal, etc.) and has added to their meaning by extending them in two different directions, all the while attempting to maintain their unity as well. Freud's original stages illuminated for the first time the bodily aspects of human development and focused on this aspect in a consistent and determined way, thereby achieving insights which a broader approach could never reach. What had been overlooked by an age which overvalued intelligence and will was brought to the fore and human development began to take on a different meaning. Childhood bodily patterns were seen as persisting into adulthood and shaping it to a greater extent than had been believed before. Freud's insistence that the body and bodily experience be attended to changed radically notions of adulthood and maturity which previously had neglected this aspect.

Erikson's gratitude for the contributions of Freud is obvious in his work and he uses these insights quite deliberately as the basis for his own work, being very careful not to deviate too far from them. However, despite his allegiance to his teacher and his principles, Erikson has broadened the Freudian notions of human development and enabled us to understand more. Beginning from the Freudian emphasis on the bodily aspect of human experience, Erikson has extended these insights in two directions (the ego and the social) while attempting to maintain the integrity of the human being in all three (the body, the ego, and the social). He makes this project very explicit in his pioneering work, Childhood and Society (1963):

> A human being, thus, is at all times an organism, an ego, and a member of society and is involved in all three processes of organization . . . We are speaking of three processes, the somatic process, the ego process, and the societal process. (p. 36)

I think it is important to note here that Erikson is careful not merely to add the ego and social aspects onto the bodily without exemplifying their integration. Were he to do so, his approach would be merely eclectic. Erikson's work is so valuable because he demonstrates the intermingling of these aspects both theoretically and in specific cases. He says what many others have said (e.g., that the social must be attended to) but he does it in such a way that the various aspects flow together and the whole picture is meaningful. Basic trust, for example, includes the bodily experience of trust, the ego aspect (the predictions of what the other will do), and the social aspect (interaction with the other). It becomes difficult to speak of each aspect separately since one always implies the other two. What Erikson has accomplished is a broadening of the psychoanalytic perspective without distorting or minimizing the insights gained from this perspective.

The Omission of the Self

However, even one who is sympathetic with a psychoanalytic orientation has some difficulty staying within the bounds of the client's bodily, ego, and social aspects despite the richness of the insights gained. There is more than that to consider, especially if one places the priority on experience as lived rather than on thoughts about that experience. One may view the experience through the three-pronged approach suggested by Erikson and one may tailor the experience to fit into this theory. But, if one attends to the experience, there seems to be much that is left out. I think Karen Horney (1950) sensed this and posed the existence of a real self (p. 17) as differentiated from a neurotic self even though there is no place in psychoanalysis for something called a "real self." It was her experience, I suspect, which led her to violate the theoretical limits.

In an ideal world it might be possible to be open to all aspects of experience and obviously such openness is to be endorsed. However, being human and limited, it seems that, especially in the area of psychological theory, there needs to be a gradual, step-by-step broadening so as to retain whatever new aspects of experience have been added. Erikson's work has enabled us to be constantly mindful that the human being cannot be considered solely in bodily terms but must also be seen as an ego and as a social being. The traditional psychoanalytic insights concerning the person as bodily being are not then invalidated but they are integrated into a larger view which does, to some degree, alter them. In the same way, Erikson's approach must be broadened since he, like most psychologists, seems to overlook or to minimize what is most characteristic of human beings and that is not their bodies, their rationality, or even their relationships with others.

When do we, as human beings, experience ourselves as being most ourselves? It is true that, in such experiences, our bodies are experienced as harmonic and vitalized, but it is also true that the focus is not on the body. In fact, if we did attend to the body in such experiences, we would become self-conscious and awkward. It is also true that our rationality, the ego aspect, is often in tune and available to us in such experiences. But, there is also a way in which the experience transcends our thoughts. We may say, especially in these experiences, that we are ahead of our thoughts and it is only in later reflection that we really "know" fully what we were doing. These statements are not meant to glorify impulsivity as a mode of existence; to say that our most characteristic human activity is not completely rational does not mean that irrationality is the ideal. It is meant as a descriptive statement. It is also true that in our most authentic moments we experience greater openness to others but, even if another is involved, as in therapeutic caring, we are focused on the other and may not even be aware that we are in tune with him. However, attempts to make the social relationship the focus of our attention inevitably fail. Nothing breaks true communication faster than the injunction, "Now, let's really communicate." Obviously, all three aspects are involved but no one or combination of the three really describes what is most central in these moments.

Nor are these moments of experiencing ourselves as more fully ourselves necessarily esoteric or "far-out" experiences. They happen in ordinary life to ordinary people and there is even an ordinary language in which they are expressed. Erikson himself (1961) does an excellent job of naming these experiences as they correspond to the various developmental stages: hope, will, purpose, skill,

4

fidelity, love, care, and wisdom. Although Erikson presents these as afterthoughts or by-products of the developmental crises, I would submit that these experiences are the most central for the various developmental stages and that the bodily, rational, and social aspects accompanying them are less central although necessary. Erikson describes hope, will and so forth as "strengths" or "virtues" following upon the successful resolution of the various life crises. For many reasons, the majority of psychologists have excluded such terms from their professional vocabulary but they can represent the most significant themes with which most people are concerned, whether knowingly or unknowingly, and they can lead to a more integrated understanding.

Obviously, psychologists must set limits for their own discipline since they do not purport to study all aspects of life (the economic, the religious, the aesthetic, etc.). This necessary specialization, however, may lead to a distortion and, as I shall expand upon later, this distortion has occurred with regard to a very fundamental issue, the "who" of the person. It is my contention that psychology, in setting the limits for its own discipline, has been involved in a case of mistaken identity with regard to the human being. It has, for the most part, identified the person with the ego, the rationality, the management functions. It is precisely this aspect of the person, especially when lived as a distinctive mode, which Heidegger (1927/1962) has named "inauthenticity"; that is, not being oneself. The "strengths" which Erikson names, in contrast to ego functions, provide a truer basis for identity. Erikson (1968) correctly points this out when he says, for example, "I am what hope I have and can give" (p. 107). I am on much firmer ground when I identify myself with my hope than with my cleverness. I am more myself when I am hopeful than when I am calculative, although some calculation may also be involved in my more authentic moments.

Traditional psychoanalytic thinkers do not make the mistake of identifying the person primarily with the ego functions but it does seem to me that they distort one's identity when they identify it primarily with body and bodily experience. It is one thing to make the true statement that I am my body but it is another thing to identify myself primarily with its fluctuations and habitual inclinations

5

(oral, anal, etc.). One of the reasons for the acceptance of Erikson's ideas, I think, is that he was able to move from this narrow position by pointing to the ego and the social as also worthy of focus in understanding who the person is.

At this point I would like to make the distinction between the ego as postulated by psychoanalysis and the ego as more generally understood. Although there is agreeement that ego refers primarily to the executive capacity of the person, the functional, rational aspects, the psychoanalytical understanding is much more specialized (the id, ego, superego model) and retains the psychoanalytic emphasis on bodily experience and the unconscious with the ego very limited by this situation. Sometimes, in Erikson's work, he seems to speak of the ego in this more traditional way but more often he seems to give it greater emphasis and to stretch it to include higher realms of experience. Of course, other neo-psychoanalytic thinkers are also moving in this direction.

The ego, in traditional psychology apart from the psychoanalytic school, is much more emphasized and identified with the person. For example, decision making is seen by many primarily in terms of cognitive dissonance and information processing and little recognition is given to the ordinary experience we have of discovering that we have already decided as opposed to deciding on the basis of figuring things out. For example, two people in love usually discover that they are committed to each other rather than looking at all the advantages and disadvantages and then deciding. In fact, as I shall attempt to develop throughout this work, traditional psychology's view of the ego is a distortion, a case of mistaken identity, an unhealthy and inauthentic perspective for ordinary living. When I refer to the ego in this work, I am referring to the more common understanding, the ego as the rational, functional aspect of the person, rather than to the more specialized psychoanalytic understanding of ego. When the latter understanding is meant, I shall so indicate.

I have already made two critiques: one of psychoanalysis and another of traditional psychology other than psychoanalysis. I want to be clear that the criticism is not a refutation of the insights gained from either perspective. Both perspectives, when adopted, yield true and valuable understandings of the person. What I am objecting to is the forgetting that these are perspectives and that the perspectives tend to become totalized; that is, everything is seen from the perspective and fitted into it. In psychoanalytic thinking, and in practice, there tends to be a forgetting that the person is more than his sedimented bodily habits. In traditional psychological thinking, there tends to be a forgetting that the person is more than his rationality. These are perspectives one takes in order to see more, but they are not permanent resting places. Erikson has already broadened the psychoanalytic perspective into a broader one which has integrity, is not fragmented. By using his work and his words, I hope to point the way to an even broader one which still, however, remains a limited perspective and is subject to further expansion. The difficulty is not so much in broadening the perspective (every theory leaves something out) but to do it in such a way that the insights of this perspective are affirmed and integrated, and this is no easy task.

My criticism of the practice of totalizing the psyochoanalytic perspective, the traditional psychological perspective, or even of Erikson's three-pronged perspective stems from the fact that they all omit (although Erikson hints strongly in this direction) what is most essential to the person, his or her authentic, though always limited, selfhood. It is here that Heidegger's Care Structure is most helpful in laying the ground for a truly human psychology.

The New Paradigm: The Care Structure

In Being and Time (1927/1962) Heidegger, as a philosopher, attempted to work out the question of what it means to be by describing in a concrete way how we are. His project was not to develop an anthropology or philosophy of man and he objected to attempts to understand his work in this way. However, as a psychologist, I have found much of his work valuable in understanding human existence and, more specifically, human development. In fact,

7

he makes the point repeatedly that human existence cannot be understood unless it is considered within the horizon of time. Another way of saying this, for me, is that human psychology cannot be understood unless it is considered within the framework of developmental psychology. The human being always has some relationship to time—to his past, present, and future—and this relationship is central to his existence. Whether or not a person is an introvert, for example, is less important than the way that person is toward his/her past, present and future.

The Care Structure, according to Heidegger, expresses "the fundamental characteristics of Dasein's Being" (1927/1962, p. 293) and this structure will provide the framework within which Erikson's contributions will be considered. (The term "Dasein" is used by Heidegger in order to avoid the misunderstandings accompanying the word "self"; it represents a new understanding of the person.) The Care Structure itself has three fundamental characteristics (Heidegger, 1927/1962): "The fundamental ontological characteristics of this entity (Dasein) are existentialiity, facticity and Being-fallen" (p. 235).

> The ontological signification of the expression "care" has been expressed in the "definition": ahead-of itself, Being-already-in (the world) as Being-alongside entities which we encounter (within-the-world). In this are expressed the fundamental characteristics of Dasein's Being: existence, in the "ahead-of-itself"; facticity, in the "Being-already-in"; falling, in the "Being-alongside." (p. 293)

The language of Heidegger is very specific and exact with regard to his project and one hesitates to use a different language to express these themes. But the risk of distortion and misunderstanding must be taken if a psychologist is to profit from Heidegger's vision of human existence.

Facticity

The person is fundamentally characterized by facticity, fallenness and existentiality. Facticity (Being-

8

already in) refers to the fact that the person finds
himself or herself already in a situation, already
within limits, having a past, having been born into a
certain tradition, family, social class, being male
or female, and so forth; in sum, this characteristic
refers to all the limits within which the person may
be free. No person has unlimited freedom and this
characteristic refers to those limits. I think
Erikson (1969) acknowledges this characteristic of
human existence when he says about Gandhi:

> For membership in a nation, in a
> class, or in a caste is one of those
> elements of an individual's identity
> which at the very minimum comprise
> what one is never not, as does
> membership in one of the two sexes or
> in a given race. What one is never
> not establishes the life space within
> which one may hope to become uniquely
> and affirmatively what one is. (p.
> 266)

Facticity refers primarily to the past, but, for
human beings, the past is not linear and set but is
constantly being worked out along with the present
and the future. Traditional psychoanalytic thinking
has been aimed primarily at this characteristic of
existence and has illuminated many of the ways in
which we are limited by our past. Binswanger (1963)
expands upon this point in seeing the unconscious as
a manifestation of the person's facticity:

> The thrownness of the Dasein, its
> facticity, is the transcendental
> horizon of all that scientific
> systematic psychiatry delimits as
> reality under the name of organism,
> body (and heredity, climate, milieu,
> etc.) and also for all that which is
> delimited, investigated and re-
> searched as psychic determinateness:
> namely, as mood and ill humor, as
> craziness, compulsive or insane
> "possessedness," as addiction, in-
> stinctuality, as confusion, phantasy
> determination, as, in general, uncon-
> sciousness. (pp. 212-213)

The person never begins with a clean slate; all the ways in which one already finds oneself being at a particualar time are included under the term "facticity."

It seems to me there are three dangers in thinking about this characteristic. One danger is to focus on facticity or certain manifestations of it as the main characteristic of human existence. Here a perspective becomes the perspective, as seems to have occurred with traditional psychoanalytic thinking. Erikson's broadening of this focus to include the ego and the social has been a very important corrective to this tendency. The second danger is to see facticity as apart from the other characteristics of human existence and as a static thing. The past, for example, is not static and depends to a large extent on how I am in my present and toward my future. For example, if I am being sentimental, I tend to be reminiscent about my past; if I am resolute, the past takes on a different character and, even, content. A third danger is to see facts about human beings as if they were facts about things. This danger is counteracted well by the saying of a colleague of mine, "A man is not bald in the same way as a cue ball is." To avoid these dangers and to see persons more in their fullness, as Heidegger does, is no easy task.

Fallenness

Erikson, sensing the narrowness of focus of traditional psychoanalytic thinking, moves toward the inclusion of the person's ego in his framework. Although he generally stays within the more specialized psychoanalytic understanding of ego, it is a definitive move to include the controlling, manipulative aspects of the person. Persons are not wholly defined by facticity but have some control over the different situations in which they find themselves. For each stage of development, Erikson points to the specific ego function, using words such as self-control, direction, and technique. Traditional American psychology, with its pragmatic, action-oriented emphasis, unlike psychoanalysis, has always highlighted this aspect of the person. Cognitive approaches and decision-making appproaches are particularly representative of this emphasis.

Heidegger uses a curious term to express the ego aspect of the person; namely, Being-fallen or fallenness. By this term he means the typical way in which we are occupied by the daily events of life, our everyday tasks, and the way in which this involvement enables us to avoid confronting some other basic issues, such as the issue of death. Rather than seeing the rational, technical person as the ideal, as tends to be the case in American psychology, Heidegger calls this mode inauthentic, meaning that it is precisely in this aspect that we are not ourselves. On the other hand, he does not take a moralistic view here since fallenness and inauthenticity are essential characteristics of being human. This is the way things are. The second fundamental characteristic of being human is fallenness.

In addition to finding ourselves already in situations, already limited, it is also true that we have some control and can figure things out and do things. If we find ourselves lonely, for example, we can find techniques of "winning friends and influencing people." We can also establish new habits; jogging is said to be a most effective "cure" for depression. We can use our heads so as not to become involved in "no-win" relationships, and so on. This ego-functioning is an essential aspect of being human and has its place in the total picture. However, the totalization of it or the primacy of it in human living can be described as inauthentic or what Heidegger calls living in the "they." "They," the public or the latest fad, say that technical solutions should be found for whatever problems we have, including those created by technology in the first place.

In this framework of human development, the ego aspects of prediction and control, for example, are seen as essential aspects of being human. However, our culture so prizes these aspects that it is difficult for us to see anything beyond that. Whenever I discuss modes such as hoping or willing, the one most frequently asked question is "How to," how to be hoping, willing and so on. This tendency to make the technical primary, even in issues which are inappropriate to it, is to my mind the most difficult obstacle we have to overcome in arriving at a fuller understanding of what it means to be human. In saying this, I am not taking an anti-technical
11

attitude either. There are certain disciplines involved in therapeutic caring, for example, and these must be practiced. However, they do not "cause" therapy to take place. The most that can be said for them, and that is quite a lot, is that they can make it possible for therapy to take place by removing obstacles to it. Although we can't, by manipulating ourselves, care, we can, by developing certain practices, stop our usual ways of not caring, thereby making it possible that caring will happen. When we look for a technique which will make us successful at caring, we are being-fallen or inauthentic and this is an essential aspect of being human.

The temporary mode characterizing the state of fallenness is the present. The concern with our everyday business, its strategies and techniques often brings with it the attitude that the present-oriented concerns that we have are the most vital issues. In our calculations we may even try to make a present "high" last longer and even "work" at that. If, for example, we had a "peak experience" in encountering a beautiful view of nature, we may try to recreate it thereby making it less likely to happen. In this mode, which Heidegger describes as living a series of "now" moments, the future is also seen in this way as an extension of the present. What is not confronted is the fact that these "nows" end, that human existence comes to an end, that we die, and that we die alone. It is especially important, in discussing human development to keep this in mind, not in a morbid way, but as the context within which it is to be considered.

Existentiality

At the same time that we find ourselves already limited, both in ourselves and by the situation and at the same time that we are constantly falling into inauthenticity, there is a third fundamental characteristic of being human which Heidegger points out and that is the mode of the possible; he calls this characteristic "existentiality." Both psychoanalytic approaches and other traditional approaches have excluded this characteristic from consideration primarily because its open-ended nature does not lend itself to natural scientific research methods. However, if one does not limit oneself to this narrow view of science and if one accepts

disciplined phenomenological description as a valid
scientific method, it does become possible to address
this characteristic of human living and to point to
some of its essential themes.

The framework proposed here should not be
confused with some humanistic approaches which
idealize and romanticize this characteristic of human
existence. In those views the person is seen as
having unlimited possibilities and the factical and
fallen characteristics are ignored. Such exclusive
emphasis on one characteristic is just as open to
criticism as psychoanalysis' exclusive focus on the
factical character of the person and it fosters
dangerous illusions rather than facing the issues of
existence. For Heidegger, human existence is not
pure possibility but thrown (factical) possibility,
embodied, finite, limited. One's possibilities must
be seen within their proper context. As Gelven
(1970) points out:

> The awareness of death points out one
> of the most persistent doctrines of
> Heidegger's philosophy that
> possibility means more than merely a
> future actuality. As a human being I
> live in the realm of possibilities--
> and it is in the realm of
> possibilities that authentic
> existence is realized. (p. 157)

Authentic living is related most directly to the
characteristic of existentiality. I am not authentic
in merely surrendering to the facticities of my life,
not in calculating and busying myself in a fallen way
but in the discovering and creating of my possibilities. In these moments and in this mode I am most myself. I think it is important not to identify a
client, for example, with his neurotic meanderings
but to be alert to those moments when he is being
himself and to respond to him in his possibilities.
If this characteristic is not acknowledged in psychological theorizing, we are in danger of missing what
is most meaningful about the client, his hoping,
willing, imagining, and so on. The main difference
between the proposed framework and other psychological approaches lies in the fact that not only is the
characteristic of existentiality included but it is
the integrating theme for an understanding
of the human person. What is most
strikingly absent in other approaches, or, in

Erikson's case, merely hinted at, is the characteristic of possibility, of future, which in Heidegger's Care Structure has the highest priority (Gelven, 1970): "The future is the most determinate and significant of the three ekstases and Dasein's basic focus of meaning is future" (p. 189).

There are some other psychologists who have developed theories along similar lines. For example, corresponding to the characteristics of facticity, fallenness, and existentiality, Viktor Frankl (1969) has used the terms: biological, psychological, and noological (the latter referring to the realm of meaning). Adrian van Kaam's self theory (1981) uses the terms: vital, functional, and transcendent. This distinction between the functional ego and the authentic self is basic for the new paradigm and I think it is very much in harmony with Heidegger's thinking. Too often, psychology has been involved in a case of mistaken identity, confusing the ego which is the person's inauthenticity with the authentic self. It should be remembered that we are not two selves and that inauthenticity is essential to our identity but to identify ourselves exclusively with it is to make a radical and basic error. These points will be elaborated in the treatment of the more specific issues faced at each stage of development.

Being-with

In addition to broadening the framework of psychoanalysis toward the ego, Erikson has attempted to include the social as well. This attempt is much in harmony with Heidegger since he sees the social as essential to human existence and as a necessary ingredient in any reflections on human existence. Heidegger considers the social in terms of Being-with (Gelven, 1970):

> To say that Being-with (or to be-with) is an a priori existential of Dasein means that one cannot be a self unless it is within one's possibilities to relate in a unique way with other Daseins. Hence to be Dasein at all means to-be-with. (p. 68)

14

Despite this statement, however, I think that Erikson
has highlighted the importance of the social in more
concrete terms. Heidegger's emphasis was more on the
single person and his or her relationship to Being.
In this framework we will use the terms "others"
and/or "the world" rather than "Being" to point out
this essential relationship.

Summary of the Approach

Having come this far, I think we are now in a
position to outline in a summary way the general
intent of this work. The traditional psychoanalytic
treatment of development focused almost exclusively
on body and bodily experience (oral, anal, etc.).
Erikson has broadened this view of development by
including the psychoanalytic sense of ego and the
social and his approach could be outlined in the
following schematic way.

Figure 1. Erikson's neo-psychoanalytic approach

This work is an attempt to broaden Erikson's view in
the light of the Care Structure which, according to
Heidegger (1927/1962, p. 293) expresses "the
fundamental character of Dasein's Being." It is
schematically presented in the following way:

Figure 2. The broader paradigm

Note. The asterisk is used to indicate that the
existential is the primary mode of existence.

The arrows represent the relationship of co-
constitution which the person has with others and the
world; that is, the person is constituted by them and
also constitutes them; they make the person be in
certain ways and the person makes them be in certain
ways. The person is not completely determined by
others and the world nor does he or she have complete
control over them; it is a mutual co-constitutive
relationship. Included on the side of the person are

the fundamental characteristics of facticity, fallenness, and existentiality. The facticity represents the "thrown" characteristics of the person. The person was thrown into this body, this family, this culture, this time in history, and so forth, and this is an essential aspect of each person.

In Heidegger's sense, fallenness has to do with the necessary ways in which we become lost in the "they," forgetting our own views and conforming to society's views. In this sense, it could be represented as the world or others determining the person ($W \rightarrow P$). Psychologically speaking, I take the view that the opposite of something is the same as it, that opposites participate in the same mode of existence. Although this is stated boldly so as to highlight the difference between a natural science and a human science, the following chapters will demonstrate the truth of it. If one is being passive and conforming without taking a stand toward the other, one can predict that the opposite (defiance, rebellion) is lurking there also and is likely to occur. For this reason, I include in fallenness the two modes: $W \rightarrow P$ and $P \rightarrow W$; the second representing the egoistic demands made on the world and others, the prediction and control, manipulation, and so on, which is involved in this relatinship. Both of these modes are in contrast to $W \leftrightarrow P$, the harmonic, mutual relationship which characterizes our more authentic moments. The two modes noted above are characteristic of everyday inauthentic relationships.

The third fundamental characteristic of human existence is that of existentiality; it is the most important of the three but must always be considered in unity with the other two. The mode of human authenticity always operates within the factical and fallen limits and never ideally. It is a vulnerable human being who is hopeful or courageous, one who, for the most part, lives in routine conformity and not some perfect being. This fundamental characteristic of human existence has not even been included in most psychologies and it is the most basic contribution of a Heideggerian approach. Human existence is not accurately seen unless these three characteristics of the person are included in an integral way nor is it accurately depicted unless the person's relationship with the world and others is included in this overall framework.

16

The way in which we will proceed is to take each of the developmental crises described by Erikson and to see them within this broader framework. Obviously, this framework has not been worked out in every detail and represents a way of proceeding rather than a finished product. At each stage, the traditional psychoanalytic view of development (oral, anal, etc.) will be understood as one aspect of a person's facticity, his biological facticity, keeping in mind that there are other determinations, some of which will be pointed to. The more biologically-centered statements of Erikson will also be seen in this way. The crises named by Erikson (trust vs. mistrust, etc.) will be understood as representing his three-pronged approach and, in the outline form, will be placed between facticity and fallenness. With some modifications, we will take advantage of some terms used by Erikson in another context to characterize the fallen and existential characteristics of each stage of development. The terms under fallenness include those which represent ego control, such as control, direction, method. The terms under existentiality are those which represent an open-ended, future-oriented, authentic mode of existence, such as hoping and caring. On the world pole of the self-world relationship we will include Erikson's depiction of the social for each stage of development.

The general framework may be outlined schematically in this way:

Figure 3. The broader paradigm in more detail

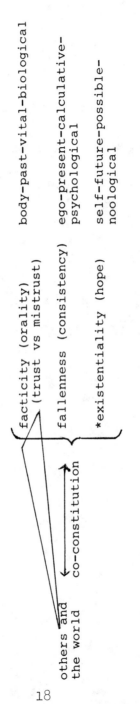

others and the world
co-constitution

facticity (orality)   body-past-vital-biological
(trust vs mistrust)

fallenness (consistency)   ego-present-calculative-
                           psychological

*existentiality (hope)   self-future-possible-
                           noological

Note. The terms in parentheses refer only to the first stage of development and are offered as examples. All other terms refer to all stages of development.

18

The triangle represents Erikson's approach. The spirit of this work is to affirm the traditional psychoanalytic contributions to development and Erikson's contributions as well but to see them in this broader context, putting the emphasis on existentiality as the missing integrating principle. Neat outlines, however, don't guarantee accuracy. Let us proceed to the first stage of development using as a criterion not how well these reflections fit into a predetermined scheme but how truly they reflect our experience.

CHAPTER TWO

HOPING

A schizophrenic patient lives in constant terror, beset by horrible fantasies. An alcoholic dimly perceives that to continue drinking would mean his death. An office worker is constantly analyzing the "political" situation there to see whether or how he will be hurt. A student is fearful about presenting a paper to his class. And, finally, a dying mother impresses everyone with her courage and concern for her children and their welfare.

I hope to show in this chapter how the situations named above may be understood more fully when seen as related to the first crisis or issue of development. It may seem strange to see these situations as related to the first year of life, as if we were saying that the person merely repeats the same issue over and over throughout life. This sort of contention could be dismissed easily as a naive and literal psychoanalytic interpretation which violates our own experience of ourselves. However, it is also true that our first experience of something is paradigmatic for us and has something to do with later experiences of a similar nature. To discount this fact would be to negate the contribution of psychoanalysis and to negate our own experience.

The decisive thing is the way in which a person's history is understood, the way in which that history participates in a person's later life. Rather than conducting a general discussion of this point, let us move into the more specific understandings of traditional psychoanalysis and of Erikson regarding the first stage of development and see how the contributions of phenomenology may enrich these insights and, more importantly, contextualize them.

Although traditional psychoanalysis identifies the first year of life as the oral stage and Erikson sees the crisis of this stage as between basic trust and mistrust, we will consider the issue of hoping as being central. This term, also the title of the chapter, was identified by Erikson (1961) as being the "virtue" (meaning strength) related to the experiences of this stage. It is not that hope emerges full blown at the end of the first year of life but that the rudiments of hope are developed at this stage. Since hope is related to the first experiences of the human being, it may be characterized as the most fundamental or basic strength to be considered. As will be discussed later, hope means simply openness. The most fundamental issue is a matter of perception. Obviously, no one of us is completely open to the world and other people. The paradigmatic experience of our first encounter with others has something to do with the degree of openness or closedness we display in later life.

Orality: An Aspect of Facticity

The traditional psychoanalytic treatment of orality is a description of the ways in which we are closed due to our early bodily experience, the ways in which our perception is limited. In our terms, since there are always limits to our openness, psychoanalysis describes the limits within which each of us may be open. In contrast to psychoanalysis, we would not identify the person with his limits (for example, an oral personality) but, on the other hand, the fact of those limits cannot be ignored. By emphasizing bodily experience, psychoanalysis has made the great contribution of keeping us honest. Hope and openness are experienced bodily or not at all. To claim to be open in the presence of bodily tension or even to claim that there are no limits to our openness, as some humanistic approaches do, is to ignore the contributions of psychoanalysis and to distort our own experience. It is our view that the limits are there, that some of them stem from our early biological experience but also that we and our experience are open-ended.

Figure 4. The person as limited openness to the world and others

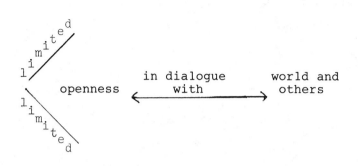

openness   in dialogue   world and
                 with   others

Erikson recognizes limits other than those stemming from our early individual psychological relationships; here again the social dimension is integrated into this psychoanalytic understanding.

It is the contention of psychoanalysis, and a familiar one by now, that the ways in which we experience oral gratification in the first year of life have determining effects on our later experience. It does make sense that the infant, not yet rational and somewhat chaotic, dependent for his or her life on another, would establish some deep-rooted, practically unshakable patterns of gratification and that these patterns would influence future forms of relating. Much has been written about these facticities so I won't go into them further here except to note that the emphasis is on that part of the body which is most visible and active; namely, the mouth, which is spoken of as an "erogenous zone," the central means by which gratification in this stage is secured.

Horizontality: Another Aspect of Facticity

Phenomenology is sometimes spoken of disparagingly as the science of the obvious but the phenomenologist insists that the obvious is also necessary to consider. Besides the central role the mouth plays in the first year, there is another obvious fact and that is that the infant is lying down during this year, is in the prone position. We might say that, in addition to oral issues of this stage, there are also issues related to what Bernd Jager (1971) calls "horizontality." Both themes are connected with the fundamental issue of hoping.

In the horizontal position, lying on the back for the most part, the infant, according to Jager, is open to horizons and the significant figure in the horizon is the face of the mother. Jager describes a horizon as "that which calls us forth and invites us in" (1971, p. 213). In the child's helplessness, the degree to which he or she can be open has much to do with the kind of welcome received. As Jager puts it:

> There is a reassuring quality in the motherly presence which stills a child's fears. . . . A child growing up around hard faces, closed expressions, rejecting stances will find his access to the world barred. The face of the other is the portal through which we enter the world. (1971, p. 215)

It is well known that in fear perception is very narrowed and that in relaxation it is opened. Patterns of such narrowing and opening to the world and others are being established in the first year and these are patterns which precede rationality and which are formed in a life and death context.

For we cannot forget that the horizontal position is also the position of vulnerability. At no time in life are we as delicate and helpless. Since it is impossible to remember this experience exactly and since infants can't tell us about it, I asked adults to describe their experience of being in the presence of an infant. The main theme that emerged from these descriptions was an awareness of the infant's fragility; they were constituted by the infant to be careful. The way in which the infant was cared for has something to do with the patterns established for coping with vulnerability. We may get some inkling of what these patterns are by the way we react to being flat on our backs in the hospital awaiting surgery, for example. Here the issue of hope and the themes of fear, vulnerability, dependency, and so forth are reexperienced on an adult level.

What we have done so far is to identify the issue of hope or openness as being the central issue of the first stage of development. We have also uncovered some of the themes which are related to this issue: vulnerability, fear, dependency, and so on. We have also pointed to the fundamental nature of this issue; it is an issue of life and death. If the infant is not cared for or is cared for in an inadequate manner, the consequence is death. The well-known studies (Spitz, 1945; Bowlby, 1952) documenting the higher mortality rates for institutionalized children have already demonstrated what is at stake at this level of development. We don't know what kind of awareness of the closeness of death infants may have but, since even animals show some "awareness" of it in extreme situations, we may assume some kind of physical or experiential awareness of this threat.

We have been considering these themes and experiences so far as being in the nature of facticities; that is, from the point of view of the patterns or limits that have been set as a result of the ways in which the infant was cared for. Facticities are those aspects of experience over which we had no choice. Just as we didn't choose our culture, time in history and so on, we had no say over the history we lived in the first year of our lives. Psychoanalysis has pointed to some of these limitations and we have added others. At any point in our lives we are already "thrown" into a historical context, always bringing with us a particular past and it is within this context that our possibilities lie. Although we can never have a perfect understanding of these limits, we can at least recognize and appreciate the fact that they are there and include them in our theories of development. We will have more to say about the way in which these facticities operate later in the chapter but, at this point, let us consider the way in which Erikson has broadened the traditional psychoanalytic understanding of orality so as to more accurately reflect our experience of the issue of the first stage.

Trust vs Mistrust:
Erikson's Three-Pronged Approach

Erikson retains the psychoanalytic insight into the fact of one's bodily existence and keeps it central at the same time as he broadens it to include the ego and social aspects of the person. He is careful to retain his identification with the psychoanalytic tradition and so he is caeful to keep the emphasis on bodily facticity. At the same time, the terms he uses to discuss his broadened approach are terms familiar to phenomenologists and to those who also take everyday language seriously.

Erikson first of all brings out the fact that the first crisis of development includes an ego aspect as well as the bodily aspect of orality. Despite the fact that the ego is not yet formed at this time in life, he calls the basic and primitive formings of it as a crisis of basic trust and identifies it as the first task of the ego (1963, p. 249). The ego he describes is the psychoanalytic understanding of ego, a specialized term within the context of that tradition and, in that context, the trust he describes is more a sense of bodily trust. We, of course, differentiate the psychoanalytic ego from the more ordinary sense of ego and from the self, which is seen as the core of personality. So, we will use Erikson's term "trust" to refer to the psychoanalytic ego and his term "hope" to refer to the self aspect of this crisis.

Erikson (1963) tells us that the sense of trust in the infant develops as:

> The experience of a mutual regulation of his increasingly receptive capacities with the maternal techniques of provision gradually helps him to balance the discomfort caused by the immaturity of homeostasis with which he is born. (p. 247)

In the midst of a chaotic experience with life and death at stake, the building up of a consistent pattern of needs being met forms the beginning of a sense of basic trust. Since Erikson retains the psychoanalytic emphasis on bodily experience, the principle of homeostasis or balance is central to his understanding of basic trust and it is applicable to bodily functions. However, bodily existence is only one aspect of human existence and, as we shall see, the principle of homeostasis does not apply to the experience of hoping. To hope is not to strike a balance even though it presupposes a body subject to the principle of homeostasis. In any case, Erikson expands the understanding of orality to include the fact that there is gradually being built up a sense of bodily trust on the level of the ego.

In addition, there is a social dimension to the living out of this first crisis. Erikson (1963) insightfully describes the infant's first social achievement as the "willingness to let the mother out of sight without undue anxiety or rage, because she has become an inner certainty as well as an outer predictability" (p. 247). To trust means to trust oneself as well as the other and to be able to wait and it is a radically social experience. There is also a relation between the individual and social institutions regarding the issue of trust. In promoting and endorsing a sense of trust, Erikson sees religions and cosmic schemes which order and give meaning to existence as being particularly relevant. He says: "All religions have in common the periodical childlike surrender to a Provider or providers who dispense earthly fortune as well as spiritual health" (1963, p. 250). In our consideration of hope, we will also see a certain kind of waiting and of surrender which is not merely a matter of exchange or quid pro quo.

Erikson, then, maintaining the psychoanalytic focus on bodily existence, has broadened and extended the understanding of the first stage of development by conceptualizing it as a three-pronged affair: the interaction of body, ego, and social aspects of the crisis. He has renamed the crisis as one of basic trust vs. basic mistrust. He has pointed to some of the failures of basic trust, such as that found in infant schizophrenia. We will also describe this and the experience of addiction and some others which seem related to this crisis. His contribution has added greatly to our understanding of the issues involved in the first year of life and he has offered a vocabulary which bridges the gap between our experience and the specialized psychological theories purporting to reflect them.

Consistency and Predictability: The Fallen Aspect

As stated earlier, the ego mentioned by Erikson is the psychoanalytic sense of ego and we have limited our discussion to that. However, in our scheme, we are now considering the ego in its more usual sense of rationality, calculation, strategic thinking, "looking out for No. 1," and so on, and we are considering it as that aspect of the Care Structure called "fallenness." This aspect includes for us psychologically the way we shape the world and others and its opposite, the way we are shaped by the world and others. It is the cognitive aspect of the person which is sometimes mistaken for the self.

It would be most appropriate in dealing with the ego aspect to outline the contributions of Piaget with regard to the first year of life since this is Piaget's focus. Those contributions would then have to be integrated with Erikson's sense of trust and the experiences he describes and within the broader Care Structure. Such an ambition, while tempting, is much beyond the scope of this work and remains to be done. The reference may serve, however, to further pinpoint the usual meaning of ego and to distinguish it from the psychoanalytic meaning of ego.

Erikson obviously does not discuss the ego in the usual sense with regard to the first stage of development. He does, however, provide us with the vocabulary, giving us the word "consistency." We will use this word to describe the ego aspect of this stage of development and to add to it the meaning of predictability. As the infant begins to experience life-preserving patterns of feeding and being cared for, a certain consistency or predictability is achieved on the ego level and the foundations of ego functioning are established. The infant can eventually begin to predict events and to have these predictions confirmed or not. It remains, however, primarily an issue of perception since the infant is in the horizontal position and not yet moving and affecting the outcome of events in any strategic way. This ego aspect of the person is one which is the focus of American psychology (cognitive theories, information processing, etc.); however, we still insist that the person is not his psychology although his psychology is essential to his existence.

At this point, let us attempt to summarize by means of a figure what we have covered so far with regard to an understanding of the first stage of development.

Figure 5. The first stage of development

```
                    ⌠factical--orality, horizontality  - body
Others───────────┤   the psychoanalytic ego--trust
and   ⟵────⟶    ⟨     vs. mistrust
the                 │ fallen--consistency, predictability - ego
world               ⌡*existential - hope - self
```

The factical, fallen, and existential aspects
represent the Care Structure of human existence, the
asterisk signifying the primacy of the existential.
The factical aspects most relevant to the first stage
of development are those of orality and horizontality
although other factical aspects such as the family
and culture one is born into, the birth order, the
time in history, and so on are also just as relevant.
The fallen or ego aspect is on a very primitive level
at this age but a beginning sense of consistency and
predictability is being formed. The existential
aspect relevant at this age is hope which here does
not signify merely an attitude or mood but the
perception of the world as inviting which offers the
infant an invitation to live, the absence of which is
seen in those institutionalized infants who become
lethargic and die. The arrows represent the co-
constitution existing between others and the self.
At this stage one is more on the receiving end of
that constitution but the infant by its presence also
constitutes others. The triangle represents
Erikson's three-pronged approach to this stage of
development, an approach we are attempting to broaden
in order to make it more reflective of our experience
as we experience it. We will now move on to
phenomenological researchers and thinkers to see what
they have to contribute to an understanding of the
issues of this stage and to judge whether the
distinctions hold and whether or not our
understanding is enhanced.

Three Kinds of Trust:
Factical, Fallen, Existential

What does this model mean for the practitioner
who is constantly dealing with issues of trust,
vulnerability, openness and so on? How are these
issues lived out in adulthood and later life? What
are the implications for practice? Phenomenology
focuses on the person's experience as it is lived and
described and bases its concepts on that experience.
In that spirit Gratton (1975) undertook a phenomenol-

ogical study of the experience of interpersonal trust. She asked people to describe experiences of trust they had had and attempted to arrive at the common constituents revealed in these descriptions. One finding particularly relevant to this discussion was the discovery of three levels of trust. In the first, which we will describe as bodily trust, subjects experienced a prepersonal (unreflective) sense of bodily comfort with another person. They found themselves, their bodies, in a a relaxed nondefensive posture toward the other person without even thinking about it or being aware of it (until asked). This bodily aspect of trust we identify with the facticity of our existence; that is, due to my early bodily experience with others, particularly with my mother, it is a given that I feel comfortable and trusting of some people and not of others. I find myself trusting or not trusting without the intervention of my ego or my understandings. This trust is prerational, prepersonal, nonreflective and constitutes for me the bodily aspect of the experience of trust. I am not responsible for it, cannot take credit or blame for it; it is a fact of my history and development.

There was a second kind of interpersonal trust described by subjects. In this kind the other person was trusted because he was consistent. This kind of trust we equate with the rational, calculative, or ego aspect. I trust because I can predict the other's response. Here we see evidence of a healthy ego but, at the same time, there is something disturbing. We will make a distinction later between using one's head in the service of a value and relying exclusively on one's calculations, the latter being described as neurotic or inauthentic.

In the third kind of trusting experience described by subjects, there is a further difference. These subjects described experiences in which they were vulnerable, in which there was a risk involved, and in which they couldn't predict the other person's response. Yet they trusted anyway, chose to be vulnerable and took the risk. We identify this kind of trusting with the existential aspect and prefer to call it hope to distinguish it from Erikson's more specialized meaning of trust.

We understand hope according to the Care Structure as follows: It is a fact that I am bodily predisposed to trust or not to trust and I am constantly falling into a form of socially sanctioned ego control with regard to my trusting; in the face of this, I am open to the other in a trusting way. Another way of stating it would be; my past and my bodily experience in the past limits and sets bounds to my trusting: my calculations in the present threaten to make my trusting exclusively a matter of prediction; in the face of this, I am still able to be open to a possible future, to horizons beyond horizons. This temporal aspect will show itself more clearly when we discuss the pathologies and inauthentic everyday experiences with regard to hope. For now, though, we can see more clearly how trust and hope are lived in later life, how the limitations and possibilities of them are operative, and how we need to become clearer on these issues.

Traditional psychoanalysis points out, and correctly so, the influence of the bodily past on our capacity to hope; Erikson brings out the necessity of including the social and ego aspects in understanding hope; phenomenology affirms these and integrates them into a structure which adds another aspect as the central integrative one, the structure of the self, of possibility, a futural dimension which is always in dialogue with another or something outside the self. Let us now move to the reflections of Gabriel Marcel in order to become clearer on the existential dimension of hope and to see how the other aspects may be integrated into this broader understanding.

Hope: The Existential Aspect

There are no studies by psychologists on the experience of hope that I know of although sometimes the word itself slips into psychological discussions. It is one of those words which have been excluded from serious discussion because of the natural scientific bias present in American psychology. In fact, all the terms suggested by Erikson which have been used as the chapter titles in this work have suffered a more or less similar fate. Giorgi (1970), for one, has been critical of this narrowness and has suggested the way to a more inclusive human science. We can all describe experiences of hoping which we have had; yet, most of us have not examined these experiences in a careful and critical way. Marcel's Homo Viator: Introduction to a Metaphysic of Hope (1962) offers a rich descriptive-reflective approach to the understanding of this experience and I hope to show the light it may shed on the experiences of the first stage of development.

First of all, we must make the distinction between hope and the mood or attitude of optimism; Marcel sees hope as transcending both optimism and pessimism. We would see optimism and pessimism as being connected with the factical, bodily aspect of a person's existence, as being largely due to one's past experiences, and as lacking some of the essential constituents of the experience of hope. Whether one finds oneself in an optimistic mood or tries to talk oneself into it, there is lacking that fundamental openness to things and people as they are. Marcel (1962) expresses it this way:

> There is a purely sentimental optimism and an optimism with pretentions to reason (which to tell the truth is perhaps merely a camouflaged sentimentality) . . . When we come down to a final analysis, the optimist, as such, always relies upon an experience which is not drawn from the most intimate and living part of himself, but, on the contrary, is <u>considered from a sufficient distance</u> to allow certain contradictions to become alternated or fused into a general harmony. . . . In parenthesis we note that there is a pessimism which is the exact counterpart of such optimism. It is oratorical in the same way, and there is no fundamental distinction between them. They are like the inside and the outside of the same garment. (pp. 33-34)

So, we can see that optimism cannot be equated with hope; there is more at stake in hoping than that.

There is a second distinction to be made and that is between hope and the predictability we mentioned as the fallen or ego aspect of this stage of development. In Gratton's (1975) study, those who trusted because they relied on their predictions of the other's behavior are examples of this approach. Even though hope includes a certain kind of rationality and prediction, it cannot be reduced to it. Marcel (1962) expresses it even more strongly: "Hope and the calculating faculty of reason are essentially distinct and everything will be lost if we try to combine them" (p. 65). Hope is not the experience of:

> somehow chaining reality down in advance as one binds a debtor with the agreement one forces upon him. But we have never ceased to insist that this claim, this presumption, is definitely foreign to hope which never stipulates the carrying out of a certain contract. (p. 55)

To live out one's future exclusively on the basis of probabilities is to be so rational as to be irrational. In choosing a career or mate, for instance, predictions and probabilities should be included in the process but there is always something beyond the reasons one can give.

We have already mentioned that the first crisis of development, the crisis of hope, is a life-death matter, that it involves the question of our being able to see possibilities in the presence of our own vulnerability. Marcel (1962) discusses the close relationship which exists between hope and the tendency to despair: "There can strictly speaking be no hope except when the temptation to despair exists" (p. 36). "It seems as though it [despair] were always capitulation before a certain _fatum_ laid down by our judgement" (p. 37).

> To capitulate, in the strongest sense of the word, is not only, perhaps is not at all, to accept the given sentence or even to recognize the inevitable as such, it is to go to pieces under this sentence, to disarm before the inevitable. It is at bottom to renounce the idea of remaining oneself, it is to be fascinated with the idea of one's destruction to the point of anticipating this very destruction itself. (pp. 37-38)

Those instituionalized infants described by Spitz (1945) and Bowlby (1952) would seem to be shocking examples of such despair. Those concentration camp prisoners described by Frankl as walking around as though they were dead would seem to be others. The occasion for hope is the sensing of one's vulnerability to death, illness, and so on, but it is also the occasion for despair. The central question in the first stage of development and in later experiences of this crisis is whether, in being tempted to close off one's life and possibilities, one is able to be open enough to see possibilities for the future. In the way in which the infant experiences the first year of life, a model is being formed for facing future crises. This model is not absolutely determinative of the way in which future crises will be faced but its impact cannot be denied. I think this will become clearer as we discuss the case of a schizophrenic child.

I think it is fairly obvious that fear is centrally involved in this first crisis. (We will use the general term "fear" to cover specific fears, general fears, anxiety, basic anxiety, and so on for the purpose of brevity and in order to deal with the major aspects of the crisis.) In fact, we may say that the fundamental crisis involves the way in which we will be toward our fear and vulnerability, whether hopeful or not, whether open or closed, despair representing a final stage of fear. Marcel (1962) again discusses fear and a term familiar to modern psychologists; namely, "acceptance."

> It is obvious that in hope there is something which goes infinitely further than acceptance, or one might say more exactly, that it is a non-acceptance, but positive and hence distinguishable from revolt. . . . How, if I do not accept can I avoid tightening myself up, and, instead, relax in my very non-acceptance? We can begin to see the solution of this strange problem by reflecting that tightening up, on whatever physical or spiritual level we may be considering it, always suggests the presence of the same physical factor, which, if not exactly fear, is at any rate of the same order, a concentration of the self on the self, the essence of which is

34

probably a certain impatience. If we
introduce the element of patience
into non-acceptance we at once come
very much nearer to hope . . . the
secret affinity between hope and
relaxation. (pp. 38-39)

Some of the psychological implications of these
statements will be brought out later in this chapter.

We have been discussing hope as the major issue
of the first crisis of development and have been
attempting to become clearer about its meaning. We
have distinguished it from an automatic bodily trust
or an optimist attitude (facticity). We have also
distinguished it from the calculation of probabilities or hypothesis-testing (fallenness). In doing
so, we have been careful to point out that the factical (body, past) and the fallen (ego, present) are
essential elements to hoping. Hope is embodied; that
is, it occurs along with a relaxed body, or it is not
hope at all. Hope takes into account probabilities
and predictions, it is not irrational. But at the
same time, we have said that hope goes beyond these
two modes and we have described some of the issues
involved.

Hope has also been described as the existential,
self, or futural aspect of this stage and this
description is found in the thoughts of others as
well. Josef Pieper (1963), for example, speaks of
the structure of hope in this way:

In its fusion of positive and
negative, of ignorance on the way to
further knowledge, wonder reveals
itself as having the same structure
as hope, the same architecture as
hope--the structure that
characterizes philosophy and indeed,
human existence itself. We are
essentially viatores, on the way,
beings who are "not yet." Who could
claim to possess the being intended
for him? "We are not," says Pascal,
"we hope to be." And it is because
the structure of wonder is that of
hope that it is so essential to human
existence. (p. 104)

35

Even in such a divergent thinker as the European Marxist, Ernst Block, the centrality of the human experience of hoping is found. David Gross (1972) describes his work thus:

> Let us begin by man hoping. As Block views him, man is not given man--not man as the sum of his current attributes--but man-on-the-way to something beyond himself. He can be said to have an "essence," but the core of that essence is not static or "thick." In fact, it has not even been substantially defined as yet because it is an unfinished essence still on the way toward realizing itself. Man has not already been grasped and pinpointed; rather he is still open, still on the way to becoming what he potentially is. And the form this openness takes when man becoms his own project is hope: hope that he can become what he is not yet. (p. 116)

I think it is obvious from such statements why the experience of hope has been excluded from psychological consideration. The methodologies employed by psychoanalysis or by traditional American psychology have not been adequate to handle the open-ended nature of our most crucial human experiences, so they have acted as though these experiences do not or should not exist. The descriptive methodology of phenomenology is much more adequate to the task. If our models do not match the experience, we should change our models and that is what phenomenology is about.

In this chapter so far we have viewed the first crisis of development through the blinders of traditional psychoanalysis in which the bodily experience of orality is central. We have viewed it through the blinders of Erikson's perspective in which the experience of somatic-psychological-social trust was central. We have expanded these viewpoints into a larger structure in which the experience of hope is central and which adds to Erikson's three-pronged approach the existential or self aspect. One is more truly oneself in hoping than in fearing, predicting, and so forth, and we have tried to describe some of the issues involved in the experience of hoping. It is time to become more specific and to see how the failures of hope encountered in treatment may be understood in this broader context.

Since the first stage of development is the most fundamental, crises having to do with the issues of this stage are the most serious. We will be describing forms of psychosis, neurosis, and everyday inauthentic modes of existence which represent failures of hope. We will exemplify the particular syndromes which are related to the issues of this stage and try to show that they focus on the factical or fallen aspects of existence as central rather than on the existential. The modes of infantile schizophrenia and the addictive modes will be seen as centering on past, body, or limits; the paranoid neurotic and everyday inauthentic modes of fear-fantasy, self-consciusness, and so on as centering on present, ego concerns. We have already described hope, the authentic living of these issues, as focusing on the existential aspect as central.

It should be mentioned here that our use of the word "authentic" means specifically the living out of the existential aspect; for this stage, the living out of hope. Following Heidegger, we assert that there are no completely authentic people, that we exist for the most part in everyday inauthentic modes and that authenticity is a modification of inauthentic modes of existence rather than an ahistorical event. We have experiences of ourselves as authentic when we are hoping, willing, imagining and so on and these moments, although the most important expressions of our "selves," quickly fall into the realm of habit, routine, and our favored inauthentic modes. The term "inauthentic" is not meant in a morally or ethically pejorative sense but merely in a descriptive one. These are simply the ordinary ways in which we experience ourselves as not being ourselves; for example, in self-consciousness. So we are ordinarily behaving inauthentically. When the issues present themselves in the form of a crisis, an authentic response is possible but not necessary. We are inauthentic when the fallen aspect is lived as central. In this we are either being controlled by the world and others (World —→ Person) as in passivity or attempting to control the world and others (Person —→ World) as in manipulation. We shall see this issue more clearly when we describe the fallen aspect with regard to this stage.

Schizophrenia: A Factical Mode

But, first, we want to study the most pathological and most negative outcome which may result from a confrontation with the issues of the first stage. Here we will follow Erikson's lead when he suggests that "the absence of basic trust can best be studied in infantile schizophrenia" (1963, p. 248). He says further:

> If we ascribe to the healthy infant the rudiments of Hope, it would, indeed, be hard to specify the criteria for this state, and harder to measure it; yet he who has seen a hopeless child, knows what is not there. (1961, p. 153)

Using Bettelheim's description of "Joey: The Mechanical Boy" (1959) as our example, what strikes us is the vicious circle of fear and fantasy and the exclusion of the ego and existential aspects, with the past limiting greatly the present and the future. Bettelheim writes the case history of a schizophrenic child who converted himself into a machine because he did not dare to be human. The fantasy of being a machine, a not uncommon one among schizophrenic children today, according to Bettelheim, is obvious in this case. He says:

> Not every child who possesses a fantasy world is possessed by it. . . . Disturbed children are not always able to make the return trip; they remain withdrawn, prisoners of the inner world of delusion and fantasy. In many ways Joey presented a classic example of this state of infantile autism. (1959, p. 3)

Along with the fantasy, a fearful mode typified his behavior: "Joey had created these machines to run his body and mind because it was too painful to be human" (p. 6). Bettelheim looks for "the deep-seated fears and needs [which] underlay Joey's delusional system" (p. 6) and finally found "his despair that anyone could like him made contact impossible" (p. 8). After many years of treatment and at the age of twelve, Joey could begin to face his vulnerability and "entered the human condition" (p. 9).

In this case, the child was obviously without hope, hopeless, desparing, not open to the future in authentic possibility, and so hope was excluded or, at least, remained latent. The rational function, or the ego, rather than being oriented to the present and establishing a sense of consistency and predictability, was employed in the service of fantasy:

> If he wanted to do something with a counselor, such as play with a toy that had caught his vague attention, he could not do so, "I'd like this very much, but first I have to turn off the machine." But by the time he had fulfilled all the requirements of hs preventions, he had lost interest. (1959, p. 5)

His fear of losing his electrical current prevented him from being in the present and from using his calculative functions in the manipulation of objects present to him. In this sense, he was not in the present or had no present, except in a latent way. It was the past he was living out. His parents had treated him like a machine and he was being a machine, over and over, more elaborately each time. Embodiment which sets the limits for rationality and existentiality became more and more rigidly structured so that the limits became everything and the possible (the existential) was minimized. Even if one assumes a genetic explanation for schizophrenia, the reality of the child's life is that his facticity is paramount, as if that were the central aspect of his existence, and this is seen in adult schizophrenia as well. The situation for the adult is complicated with more advanced issues as well and, even for Joey, "anal" issues were present in a secondary way but the central issues were the issues of hope and the emphasis was on the past, body, or limits.

Laing (1965) also describes adults who experience themselves as automata, robots, bits of machinery, or even animals. He says, "The schizophrenic is desperate, is simply without hope" (the exclusion of the existential aspect) and "Schizophrenia cannot be understood without understanding despair" (p. 38). The fear-fantasy syndrome is also found throughout his description. Our understanding of this syndrome is that the presence of fear involves a tense, rigid body. The sustaining of this tightness is a physical impossibility. Release from this tightness comes with fantasy which temporarily avoids the fear but is part of the structure of it. There is a lostness of the self in fantasy and a reentry problem expperienced which serves to intensify the fear rather than lessen it. I make a distinction between fantasy and imagination. Imagination, a third stage issue, draws one into the world and is not part of the fear structure nor is it accompanied by the same bodily experiences. A similar fear-fantasy syndrome is also found in the neurotic and inauthentic modes of the first stage but it is not lived with the same centrality of facticity as in the schizophrenic mode. For example, the schizophrenic, fascinated by bodily issues, may burn himself with a cigarette to test the bodily limits whereas the paranoid character would not do so, his emphasis being on the rational.

The schizophrenic, in living the fear-fantasy syndrome, is also living a radically different mode of existence in which bodily existence itself is questionable. These descriptions of Laing give us some idea of the nature of this existence:

> What are to most people everyday happenings, which are hardly noticed because they have no special significance, may become deeply significant in so far as they either contribute to the sustenance of the individual's being or threaten him with non-being. Such an individual, for whom the elements of the world are coming to have, or have come to have, a different hierarchy of

40

significance from that of the
ordinary person, is beginning, as we
say, "to live in a world of his own,"
or has already come to do so. (1965,
p. 43)

"The individual is frightened of the world, afraid
that any impingement will be total, will be
implosive, penetrative, fragmenting and engulfing"
(p. 83). "The individual is developing a microcosmos
within himself; but, of course, this autistic,
private, intra-individual world is not a feasible
substitute for the only world there really is, the
shared world" (p. 74). The shizophrenic mode, which
is fascinated by its facticity to the exclusion of
the ego and the self, might be described as a
capitulation or a "going to pieces" in the face of
that facticity.

In this mode of existence, we can agree with
Farley (1975): "There do seem to be kinds or
qualities of assaults [on a person's vulnerability]
which are unendurable to the human being" (p. 65).
We can also see that this mode seems to belong more
to that class of experiences, such as illness, which
happen to the person although there remains a latent
ego mode and a latent self mode which may appear at
times.

Advanced Addiction: Another Factical Mode

Another mode of experience which I see as being
directly related to the life-death issues of the
firststage and which is centered on the factical
aspect of this stage is the addictive mode. In
identifying it with first stage issues, I am not
saying anything new (see, for example, Lowe, 1972, p.
260). However, in identifying it primarily with the
factical, I am. It seems fairly obvious, though,
that the addict is centered on the bodily experience
of highs and lows and with the limits of this bodily
experience. The addict's hope is minimal and his
openness to the world and others is narrowed down to
their potential as providers or withholders of the
needed substance, whether alcohol or some other drug.
The ego or rationality of the addict is likewise in
the service of the addiction and is geared to the
body as central.

In the case where the alcoholic is attempting to have the therapist collude in the denial of the problem, the theoretical understanding presented here can be helpful. Since this mode of existence is centered on the body, that should also be the focus of treatment; that is to say, no amount of talk will be helpful as long as the bodily addiction continues actively. The only hope for the addict is confrontation with the fact of the addiction and a breaking of it; only then may the ego and self aspects be appealed to. For the addict to hope or to be open to possibilities in life, there must also be the experience of being tempted to despair or, as Alcoholics Anonymous puts it, "hitting bottom," whether that bottom is the loss of face, a job, a family or, at botom, the threat of the loss of life.

This theoretical understanding of addiction is much in line with Cummings' article on this problem (1979). He says:

> There is a growing body of evidence which indicates that some people are born with a genetic predisposition to become addicted (Kandel, 1976). For others it is congenital and in utero; for example, very small amounts of alcohol imbibed by the mother during certain months of pregnancy predispose a child to alcoholism (Julian, 1978). (pp. 1120-1121)

The factical element is clearly seen here and, even if the addiction is acquired later, that is the facticity with which the addict faces the situation; that is, as an addict and not as an ordinary social drinker.

In the face of this, we agree with Cummings' statement: "The first, first, first thing one must do when confronted with an addict is convince that person that the prerequisite intervention in the addiction is abstinence from the chemical to which one is addicted" (p. 1121). Once the factical aspect is altered, then appeal can be made through insight or traditional "talk therapy." By abstaining, the person does not alter the fact of being an addict but there is a bodily modification that takes place which allows for the emergence of the ego and of the self. So, with this understanding, the therapist may, as

42

Cummings suggests, treat the addiction directly or work with the client as supplementary to the client's treatment in AA or a drug treatment center.

So, we have now identified schizophrenia and addiction as pathologies of the first stage which are centered on the factical level. Let us now turn to other problematic modes of the first stage which are centered on the fallen or ego level. In these modes fallenness is emphasized as the central aspect with a consequent minimizing of the self aspect. In both the ego and self modes the body is lived differently. However, it is only in the pathologies described above that the body is central. All aspects are present in all these modes but the emphasis is different and this emphasis affects the other two aspects as has been and will be pointed out.

The Paranoid Character: A Fallen Mode

Heidegger (1927/1962) speaks of the fallen aspct of existence as being lost in the anonymity of the "they," the crowd, Das Man, a loss of the self in the everyday concerns of life, an unreflective existence (pp. 163-168). Psychologically, we might speak of this side of the coin as being dependency, passivity, fantasy, and so on. However, there is also another side to the coin and there we might speak of individualism, activity for activity's sake, fear, and so on. In the first, the world seemingly shapes the person $(W \longrightarrow P)$; in the second, the person seemingly shapes the world $(P \longrightarrow W)$. It is our contention, based on observation of behavior, that these seeming opposites are actually different moments of one mode of existence. This is most clearly seen for example, in the case of the passive-aggressive personality. The person would be seen as passive for the most part but the aggression is also there and an essential constituent of the mode. Inferiority includes superiority, and so on. This living of the opposites as two distinct moments we call neurosis or inauthentic everyday behavior. The integration of opposites in a smooth way, such as in hope where one lives courageously despite the surety of death, we call an authentic mode. As we shall see for each stage of development, the seeming opposites are really one mode, the neurotic or inauthentic.

For the first stage, the apparent opposites are fear and fantasy. This circle has been seen even in

43

the pathologies described above; the alcoholic, for example, is found to be very timid and fearful of social situations in the sober state and may be boastful and aggressive in the inebriated state. But we are not concerned now with pathologies. We are interested in this cycle as it is lived with an accent on the ego level, where the rational is primary and the bodily and self aspects are receded. Although the pre-addictive person might be used, we see the paranoid character as most reprsentative of this fearful ego mode.

The way in which the paranoid character exhibits a lack of hope or openness to the future is through a preoccupation with the ego aspect of the first stage of development; that is, a preoccupation with consistency. He is very much involved with everyday existence, with predicting everything and checking out these predictions within his narrow, fearful horizons. As Shapiro describes him in <u>Neurotic Styles</u> (1965), "He looks at the world with fixed and preoccupying expectation, and he searches repetitively, and only, for confirmation of it [his suspicion]" (p. 56). This "sharp-eyed," "searching," "intensely concentrating" mode is in contrast to the relaxed openness of hope. This emphasis on the rational level obviously reduces hope and affects the bodily presence, making the body tense, rigid, and unspontaneous. Shapiro comments on the radical shrinking of "expressiveness or spontaneity of behavior" in this mode (1965, p. 75).

Even though a rigid body is also found in schizophrenia, the emphasis here is on a rational checking out of the fears. The paranoid character has the advantages and disadvantages of a narrowed perception. He may perceive correctly that his boss is irritable but conclude incorrectly that he is about to be fired. As Shapiro says: "The suspicious person can be at the same time absolutely right in his perception and absolutely wrong in his judgment" (1965, p. 61). This perception, although extremely realistic, is "interpretively autistic." Again the opposites show themselves: The person who is a specialist in perceiving and who makes it his life task to anticipate reality is also the most unrealistic. The basic negative emotion, as in the pathologies, is fear: "Paranoid people live in readiness for an emergency" (p. 73), "a more or less continuous state of total mobilization . . . defensive vigilance" (p.

74), "a virtual elimination of the capacity for abandonment" (p. 79). But the response to this fear is to become hyper-rational and this characteristic identifies it as an ego mode.

The paranoid neurotic is representative of the attempt of the person to shape the world (P ⟶ W) with regard to the issues of the first stage of development. Since these issues are issues of perception, the shaping that takes place is also perceptual; one shapes by predicting. This understanding of the paranoid character allows the therapist to see that it is the fear that is most basic and so the therapist addresses himself to the client's fear rather than becoming involved in the challenging of the client's perceptions or judgments. If the therapist becomes engaged in a rational argument with a specialist in rationality, the therapist will lose and will also stimulate the fear the client already has. Just as schizophrenia and addiction are the most serious of the pathologies because they deal with the fundamental issues of hope, so is the paranoid the most serious neurotic condition and the therapist should know what he's up against.

Everyday Fear and Fantasy:
Other Fallen Modes

Not every case of a deficiency of hope is as pronounced as the above examples. Becker, in The Denial of Death (1973), outlined the ways in which all of us turn away from the issues of our vulnerability. Perhaps most of us avoid these issues in a socially sanctioned quest for health or happiness or even the search for authenticity and take for granted the ideal of a "hassle-free" life. The Dutch psychiatrist, van den Berg, addresses this avoidance directly:

> An existence devoid of sickness lacks the stimulus to live, just as an existence devoid of mental problems degenerates into complete insignificance. Probably there is no better guarantee for a really unhealthy life than perfect health. But this only means that health and existence without conflict are not synonymous. The really healthy

> person possesses a vulnerable body
> and he is aware of this
> vulnerability. This results in a
> certain responsibility and this
> responsibility is never a matter of
> course. (1966, pp. 73-74)

As was stated earlier, there are no completely authentic people; such a condition violates our experience and the Care Structure reflective of it and included as an essential aspect of the Care Structure is inauthenticity or the ego mode. We all experience ourselves as being both inauthentic and, at times, authentic.

We also live out the fear-fantasy circle in our everyday lives. When I am afraid, I experience a tightening of the body, an increased alertness to the situation and my interpretation of the situation, if not completely wrong, is narrowed. Since I can't sustain such an attitude of tightness and alertness for long, I may daydream or fantasize about the situation and surrender myself to the fantasy in a tension-free irresponsibility. In both instances, the way I am to the future shapes my present and my past. In fearing the future, I narrow not only my future but my past, remembering only fearful events and in the present I am immobilized. In fantasizing the future, I "open it up" for anything, my past "opens up" in a confused, haphazard way, and in the present I am "open" in the same disembodied way. If the situation persists long enough, I may find myself in crisis about it and tempted to despair over it. If I can relax about it and accept the possibilities of both "success" and "failure," I may be able to confront the issues in a realistic way and discover different ways of seeing the situation. In the end, I may be able to be hopeful without tying that hope to a specific outcome. To the extent that I become preoccupied with the factical aspects of the situation or with the ego aspects, I am unable to hope. However, since these aspects are essential to my existence, it is only through them that I may reach authentic hope. In rephrasing the motto of Alcoholics Anonymous I would be able to accept the things which can't be changed (facticity), change the things which should be changed (the ego level), and be open in a receptive way to new possibilities (the self mode). Here the situation might be described as Person $\longleftrightarrow$ World (P $\longleftrightarrow$ W) which implies both

receptivity and responsibility for my side of the
dialogue.

Summary

Having come this far, we may ask, "What is
different about this conceptualization of the first
stage of development?" and "What are some of the
implications stemming from this conceptualization?"
With regard to the first question, we must keep in
mind the central intention of this project, to
restate Erikson's contributions in the light of some
existential-phenomenological themes. The aim is to
affirm these contributions and to overcome to some
degree the specialized understanding of them. In
Erikson's view, although the ego level is approached,
the beginning and end point of his deliberations is
found in the factical elements of existence,
especially as pertaining to the early biological
experience of the person. There is no need in
proposing an existential-phenomenological
understanding to negate these contributions. Such a
negation would violate the principle of embodiment so
central to this understanding. On the other hand,
there is no need to accept these contributions
uncritically. Rather, we would say that to the exent
that the early biological experience of the person
affects his later development, to that extent it sets
factical limits which must be accepted. However,
facticity is only one aspect of existence and what
must also be included is the ego aspect, the healthy
ego, the person's ability to master self and environ-
ment to some degree and the existential aspect, the
authentic understanding the person has of one's existence. In the case of the first stage of
development, we would say that the early biological
experience of the person, in addition to some other
factical elements, sets limits to an openness
to others and the world, that preoccupation with
consistency leads the person to fall into the habit
of constituting too rigidly or failing to constitute
the situation and that despite these factors, one can
be open to the future in authentic possibility, in
hope. The person moves from the fear-fantasy circle
by confronting despair and moving it through it to
hope. This conceptualization attempts to return
Erikson's specialized contribution to the lived world
without denying the advantages of his specialized
perspective.

With regard to the question of implications, there are many which could be suggested. The most central implication must be the necessity for researching the experience of hope. Such research should throw a different light on the pathologies described and point the way to different methods of treatment. A dialogue with research studies dealing with the need for consistency (authoritarianism, cognitive dissonance, etc.) might be most productive in lighting up the ego level of this stage. The experience of fear and fantasy might be relevant here. Obviously, traditional research methods are not adequate for such tasks and newer approaches, based on broader philosophical assumptions, must be discovered and used. In both research and practice, the specialized perspectives of various schools of thought must be incorporated into an integrated understanding of the first stage of development. The experience of hoping may hold the key to such an understanding since, in hoping, the factical and ego aspects of existence are included and integrated in an authentic manner.

CHAPTER THREE

WILLING

At this point in the history of psychology as a science, hoping and its synonyms (openness, tolerance for ambiguity and so on) are endorsed and spoken of very highly, sometimes almost reverently. Psychologists and lay people even speak of being committed to being open and of trying to make themselves open. From the previous chapter it should be clear that hoping is not an ego achievement, that a person cannot make himself or herself hopeful; rather, hope arises out of a crisis and, in fact, is a particular response to a particular crisis. Inviting the hope is tantamount to inviting the crisis and we are not that foolhardy. Even in the midst of the crisis one cannot make oneself hope; there are things one may stop doing, such as letting go of the fear-fantasy cycle but that can only prepare the way for hoping which may or may not happen.

Involved in the above misunderstanding of how hope arises is the issue of willing. To will oneself to hope is a violation of the developmental understanding being developed here since hope is the precondition for will. Hoping, being a first stage issue, provides the foundation for being able to will; to attempt to reverse the sequence leads to all sorts of problems, as we shall see in this chapter. Yet, there does seem to be in our consumer-oriented culture the tendency to attempt control of experiences which are not in our total control. The aim of traditional natural scientific psychology is even spoken of as the attempt to predict (first stage issue) and control (second stage issue) in contrast to the aim of phenomenological psychology, which is to understand.

So we see already two misunderstandings or misuses of will and there are more. The experience of willing or of taking a stand to what is encountered in the openness is viewed with much caution by traditional psychology and the charge of authoritarianism is lurking in the background. It would seem safer to remain open and to suspend one's stand indefinitely; in fact, client-centered therapy seems to move in that direction but there is also a stand taken there. The fact is that we lack an accurate language for the discussion of problems of will and the historical and cultural confusion concerning this issue is everywhere evident, from one-sided liberation movements to authoritarian cults.

And the social is not only outside of us but in us so that individually and personally we suffer the same confusion and it shows itself in our everyday behavior. Despite all these difficulties, however, the experience of willing one's future remains a memorable and central event for most people; they experience themselves as being more real at such times, more participative in life and more themselves. Perhaps we can work our way through some of the psychoanalytic and neo-psychoanalytic understandings of it and then broaden these understandings to one which more closely matches our experience.

Anality: An Aspect of Facticity

As we shall see, limits are involved in every crisis of development and traditional psychoanalysis describes these limits very well. Just as we are limited in our openness or hope, we are also limitd in our capacity for willing. The partiular kind of limit depends on the age of the child and the issue which is thematic at that stage. In the second year of life the child physically takes a first stand and the physical stand is accompanied by psychological and social aspects as well. Experiencing himself or herself as distinct from the mother, the child is able to say "No" and does so often. Psychoanalysis points out the way this first occasion of taking a stand is experienced has effects on the formation of characer for later life.

In describing the anal character (1908/1971), Freud uses language which is consistent with our contention that willing is the central issue of this stage of development. He says, for example:

> From the history of the early childhood of these persons one easily learns that they took a long time to overcome the infantile incontinentia alvi and that even in later childhood they had to complain of isolated accidents related to this function. As infants they seem to have been

50

among those who refuse to empty the
bowel when placed on the chamber,
because they derive an incidental
pleasure from the act of defaecation.
. . . (p. 39)

The psychological and social aspects of this first
stand are also brought out in the following
statement:

To bring obstinacy into relation
with interest in defaecation seems no
easy task, but it should be
remembered that infants can very
early behave with great self-will
about parting with stools (see
above), and that painful stimuli to
the skin of the buttocks (which is
connected with the anal erotic zone)
are an instrument in the education of
the child designed to break his self-
will and make him submissive. (p.
41)

Again, one hopes humorously, Freud brings out the
relationship between the bodily experience of this
stage and its relationship to the issue of willing,
both present and future. He says further:

At any rate, one can give a formula
for the formation of the ultimate
character from the constituent
characer traits: the permanent
character traits are either unchanged
perpetuations of the original
impulses, sublimations of them, or
reaction-formations against them.
(p. 43)

So we see here that Freud is pointing out the
limits of future acts of willing which stem from the
bodily aspect of this stage of development. Again,
we would agree with the truth of these limitations;
there is no doubt that people have different limits
with regard to this issue. In the popular television
show, The Odd Couple, Felix and Oscar are almost
prototypes of the character limits in this regard. It
is almost inconceivable to imagine the one changing
to become comfortable with sloppiness and the other
to become neat. However, we would not identify the
51

person with his or her character limits in this
regard or see the biological limits as the central
aspect of the person. Rather, as in regard to the
issue of hoping, we would see the limits as providing
the boundaries within which an open-ended willing is
possible for this particular person.

Figure 6. The person as limited willing to the world
and others

willing   in dialogue   world and
                    with   others
              ←——————————→

Felix, in this scheme, is not free to become a person
who is physically loose and flexible. Within the
limits of what he is comfortable with, however, he
can will freely and wholeheartedly. Continued
experiences of being willing may even have the effect
of relaxing the bodily tightness which is an aspect
of his facticity because human facticity is not the
same as object facticity.

In addition to the aspect of anality, there are
other determinations which arise from the first
experience of taking a stand. How that stand was
received by the parents, the support or lack of it,
the encouragement or discouragement and so on, all
are important in this first experience. If, for
example, the parent has to win totally and the chiild
is not permitted to say "No," this experience is
bound to set limits on the child's autonomy. Other
bad experiences with taking a stand, such as falling,
hurting oneself and so forth, all become part of the
child's history and facticity.

Autonomy vs Shame and Doubt:
Erikson's Three-Pronged Approach

Erikson expands Freud's insights into the second year of life to the ego aspect and the social aspect and names the ego crisis of this stage as one of autonomy vs shame and doubt. He begins, as usual, with the bodily experience and extends it towards the psychological and social constituents of this experience:

> Muscular maturation sets the stage for experimentation with two simultaneous sets of social modalities: holding on and letting go. . . . Thus, to hold can become a destructive and cruel restraining, and it can become a pattern of care: to have and to hold. To let go, too, can turn into an inimical letting loose of destructive forces, or it can be a relaxed "to let pass" and "to let be." (1963, p. 251)

He also makes the point that becomes a principle of both his and our conception of development; that is, that what was most precious in the previous stage of development must be risked in order to grow. For this stage, he expresses it thus:

> The infant must come to feel that the basic faith in existence, which is the lasting treasure saved from the rages of the oral stage, will not be jeopardized by this about-face of his, this sudden violent wish to have a choice, to appropriate demandingly, and to eliminate stubbornly. (1963, p. 252)

An implication of this state of affairs is that the crises are never completely solved but that they are resolved to the extent that one is able to risk moving into the next stage, that one's energies are expended on a newer issue. This risk is particularly clear when the young adult moves from the identity crisis to the crisis of intimacy, when the identity is secure enough to risk losing it in intimate relations.

One other point that might be added here is the

fact that the crisis is not resolved forever. Because development is a cycle or a growing spiral rather than a straight line and because we understand time as lived rather than as clock time, the issues reappear in later crises also. For example, the fear of intimacy which may appear in young people is a re-experiencing of a first stage issue (fear) with regard to a new content (adult intimacy). If the crisis intensifies enough, the young adult may end up dealing with the first stage issue as central and re-experience the issues of fear, fantasy, hope and so on. When or if a new resolution comes about, the person is then freed for the more adult issues of intimacy.

Erikson also points to a kind of pathology which might be relevant to the issues of the second stage of development, that of obsessiveness:

> For if denied the gradual and well-guided experience of the autonomy of free choice (or if, indeed, weakened by an initial loss of trust) the child will turn against himself all his urge to discriminate and to manipulate. . . . Instead of taking possession of things in order to test them by purposeful repetition, he will become obsessed by his own repetitiveness. By such obsessiveness, of course, he then learns to repossess the environment and to gain power by stubborn and minute control, where he could not find large-scale mutual regulation. Such hollow victory is the infantile model for a compulsion neurosis. It is also the infantile source of later attempts in adult life to govern by the letter, rather than by the spirit. (1963, p. 252)

So this experience of control which is the prototype for later experiences of control may be thwarted by a kind of hypnotic fascination with the process in forgetfulness of the object. In phenomenological terms we might say that the child comes up against the resistance of the world to his intentions. Instead of remaining focused on the world pole which is temporarily frustrating, the child becomes preoccupied with himself and his movements. The experience of this pseudo-control in the beginning of life may set limits for later experiences of control.

Erikson goes on to describe the experiences of shame and doubt which he sees as relevant to this stage of development. Descriptive phenomenological studies of these experiences would have much to add concerning the constituents of them without being confined within the boundaries of a particular theoretical framework. He also points to the legal institutions of society as being the most directly relevant to the issues of this stage:

> We have related basic trust to the institution of religion. The last-ing need of the individual to have his will reaffirmed and delineated within an adult order of things which at the same time reaffirms and delineates the will of others has an institutional safeguard in the principle of law and order. (1963, p. 254)

In both Freud's and Erikson's treatment of the experiences of this stage of development, the word "will" keeps cropping up. We will propose the experience of willing as the one which can include the others most appropriately. However, before doing so, let us turn to a description of the ego or fallen aspect of this stage, again using terms similar to those suggested by Erikson.

Control: The Fallen Aspect

Rather than using the exact term suggested by Erikson for this stage, "self-control," we use the term "control" because it is not limited to the subject pole of the experience. According to our view and following Erikson's lead, we look for the experience of this stage which is related most closely to the ego. Although one cannot will oneself to will, control is possible stemming from one's own efforts. The healthy ego for this stage of development is able to control both self and world to some extent and is able to call on this control for what is willed. Just as consistency and predictability were characteristic of the healthy ego for the issues of the first stage, so is control for the second stage.

Following Heidegger's Care Structure we use the term "fallen" to describe this aspect of the experience of this stage. One may fall into the practice of substituting control for the experience of willing and Erikson has already described this process in the obsessive. In our everyday involvements in the world, we also tend to reduce our commitments and relationships to the practice of control, thereby distorting their authentic meaning. That is not to say that it is possible to be perfectly willing in these involvements all the time or even to have that as a goal. We are attempting to be descriptive of the human experience of this stage in the second year of life and in later re-experiencing of these issues. And what happens is that the reduction to control is more typical of everyday behavior than the more authentic experience of willing. I will to write this and I can call on some control to bring this about; however, I, for the most part, am engaged in control rather than inspired willingness. The experience of willing is too fleeting to sustain over a long period even though it is the more fundamental experience and sustains the work. It would not be possible to write this without calling on ego control but, without willingness, this control is inadequate to the task.

Traditional American psychology emphasizes the importance of control and this is the proper emphasis of psychology. The various therapeutic aproaches urge one to take control of one's life. Behaviorism is almost exclusively concerned with the issue of control and, as noted previously, the goal of most psychological science is stated as the prediction and control of behavior. This emphasis, which is proper, is also too narrow and specialized. It overlooks, as does psychoanalysis, that whole range of experiences, such as hoping, willing, and so on, which, by definition, are not predictable and controllable. Since these latter experiences are the most central ones in our lives, it is important to include them in any human science. The ego, whose proper function is prediction and control, is not the self but is at the service of the self-world dialogue, either harmoniously or not. Later on in this chapter we will deal with those disharmonies with regard to the issue of willing.

For now, though, we return to the experience of the second year of life where the child, having rsolved to some degree the issues of hope and openness, begins to devote his or her energies to the issues of willing. He or she participates as a whole human being in this process and the social is an integral part of it. On the self side of the self-world dialogue are the factical, fallen and existential aspects of the child. There is genetically already a factical component provided by his or her bodily make-up. There is also a factical component povided by the way in which this particular culture forms the child. For example, in rural Ireland, shaming is often used in dealing with this stage of development. The anal experience outlined by Freud also becomes part of the child's facticity, a relatively unchangeable way of being toward the issues of willing. The actual experience and history of taking the first stands also becomes part of the facticity of the child. One may possibly change the later course of one's history to a different direction but one cannot alter the fact of that history. All of these things and more provide the limits within which the child, and later the adult, is able to be willing.

Erikson, in extending Freud's treatment of the bodily factical aspect of this stage, anality, moves to naming the psychoanalytic ego crisis as one of autonomy vs shame and doubt. This aspect, which obviously includes the factical aspects described above, implies a certain freedom from facticity or, at least, an understanding which differs from the deterministic one of traditional psychoanalysis; the word "autonomy" itself indicates this. He describes the movement from a passive, receptive infant to the beginnings of an autonomous child who is first able to control the bodily functions and later things, people and events. This is as far as Erikson moves on the self side of the dialogue.

We have already broadened the factical aspect beyond the one issue of anality. We have also added the ordinary psychological understanding of ego as control and named it as the fallen or ego aspect. We have also pointed to the fact that this understanding which includes both the factical and fallen is still incomplete and doesn't deal with the central existential aspect which we have called the experience of willing. The fact of its centrality is even indicated by Erikson in his statement (1968): "I am what I can will freely" (p. 114). However, Erikson tries to include this experience under the ego aspect. We, instead, see this experience as the existential, self aspect which serves as the integrating aspect for the others. In other words, when I am willing, my body and ego participate harmoniously and properly inthis experience; they are integrated in this experience. And, in the experience of willing, I am most myself, not in a narcissistic way but in a dialogal way, since there is always an object pole to my willing.

Again, we may represent the issues of this stage in a figure:

Figure 7. The second stage of development

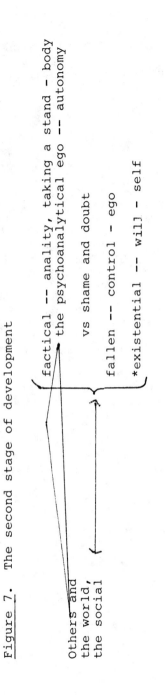

factical -- anality, taking a stand - body
the psychoanalytical ego -- autonomy

vs shame and doubt

fallen -- control - ego

*existential -- will - self

Others and
the world,
the social

Again, the triangle represents Erikson's three-pronged approach; the asterisk indicates the existential aspect as central; and, the arrows represent the fact that one constitutes others and is constituted by them.

Willing: The Existential Aspect

There is much confusion in our culture concerning the issue of will and this confusion is reflected in the fact that this is the only term of Erikson's basic virtues which had to be changed. He used the term "willpower" to indicate the basic virtue resulting from the resolution of the issues of this stage. For reasons which will become apparent later, we decided to substitute the term "willing." It is not our purpose here to settle all the theoretical confusion but we do hope to shed some light on what the confusion is about. As psychologists and as phenomenologists, our appeal is to shared experience. Rather than giving a theoretical definition of willing, we appeal to the experience of being willing to do something, of having good will, of being a willing student, worker, etc. which we observe both in others and ourselves. We don't ordinarily focus on this experience; however, if asked to describe an experience of being willing, most of us could do so readily. It is this simple experience which we see as the central issue of the second stage of development and which forms the integrating principle for the issues of anality, autonomy, control and so on.

Perhaps no other psychologist has studied this experience more closely than the Italian psychotherapist, Roberto Assagioli. He describes willing in this way:

> When we experience ourselves as "selves," as subjects, we frequently have an experience that can be summed up in this sentence: "I am a force, a cause." This is an experience of the human will. . . . We find that the discovery of the self is frequently connected with the discovery that the self has a will—is even, in a certain sense, a will. (1972, p. 91)

60

This latter sentence is reminiscent of Erikson's statement, "I am what I can will freely" (1968, p. 114).

Although we see hope as more fundamental than will and claim that it is only in the openness that one can will, we would not necessarily disagree with Assagioli's words here: "The will serves, quite simply, as the directing energy for all other psychological functions" (1972, p. 91). This central experience has been neglected by both psychoanalysis and natural scientific psychology although there are signs that this situation is changing. One of the reasons may be, as Assagioli points out: "Disgusted by the Victorian notion of the will as 'willpower,' many intellectuals joined the revolt against the will that in many ways characterized our century" (1972, p. 90). This comment and similar ones by other psychologists lead us to change Erikson's term "will-power" to "willing" since these seem to be different experiences.

Assagioli, among others whom we will quote, makes a distinction between the "right-hand path of discipline" (Victorian times) and the "left-hand path of letting go, of allowing, of release" (modern times) and makes the point that these two can be integrated in the experience of will. Neither one is an end in itself. We might add that discipline frees one _for_ whereas letting go frees one _from_ and that both are necessary for the genuine experience of will. If one focuses on the first, the openness of the first stage is lost. If one focuses on the second, one may be relatively free of inhibitions but one is still not willing. It is in the experience of willing that both are integrated and serve their proper function.

Another psychologist who addresses himself to the central question of will is Adrian van Kaam. He makes the distinction between willfulness and willlessness and the genuine experience of will. Concerning the latter, he has this to say: "I do not have a will, but I _am_ a will, or even better, I am a willing person" (1966, p. 71). And speaking of the integrating function of will, he states: "Willing is thus an expression, a mode of being of myself as a whole interacting with the totality of my life situation" (1966, pp. 71-72). Again, this is vey congruent with the model being proposed here.

Just as Assagioli speaks of the left-hand path of release and the right-hand path of discipline, van Kaam describes the two aspects of will as openness and the executive function. The first aspect is seen as an appeal, an invitation which draws the person and the second is the carrying out of what is seen as desirable. Again, the first aspect would be comparable in our scheme to the experience of hope or openness and the second to taking a stand to what appeals. Of course, this process never goes perfectly smoothly since resistances occur which also must be faced. But, when one is willing, these two constituents are observed and the experience is an experience of integration of oneself and of one's world.

Also, as Assagioli describes choice as only one of the stages of the act of will (1972), van Kaam elaborates this point further (1966):

> This most basic decision in my client is to be either open or closed to the reality of his life situation. My client is essentially free to decide one way or the other. As a human being, however, he cannot avoid the decision as such. He is not free to act. We call this decision primordial in the sense that it is prior to any judgement, practical decision, or motivation . . . The whole life of man is built upon this primordial decision. (p. 102)

We can see here that both of these psychologists avoid the narrowness of natural scientific psychologists who put information processing and cognitive decision making in the central place, ignoring the more basic experience of primordial will.

Van Kaam also differentiates the experiences of will-lessness and willfulness from the experience of willing described above. He speaks of willfulness as follows (1966):

> Willfulness is the conceited abuse of
> the second aspect of willing. We
> speak about willfulness in a person
> who tries to implement too fast, too
> impatiently, and too forcefully a
> truth which is revealed to him as the
> truth of his life. (p. 77)

Much will be lost if we identify willing with either
willfulness or the reaction against it which is will-
lessness.

As we look further into those psychologists who
have studied the experience of will, we find striking
the degree to which they are consistent. For
example, with regard to van Kaam's critique of
willfulness, Rollo May has similar things to say. He
speaks of Freud's greatest discovery as "cutting
through the futility and self-deceit in Victorian
will power" (1969, p. 182). He also stresses the
integration necessary in genuine willing:

> "Will" and "wish" may be seen as
> operating in polarity. "Will"
> requires self-consciousness; "wish"
> does not. "Will" implies some
> possibility of either/or choice;
> "wish" does not. "Wish" gives the
> warmth, the context, the imagination,
> the child's play, the freshness and
> the richness to "will." "Will" gives
> the self-direction, the maturity to
> "wish." "Will" protects "wish,"
> permits it to continue without
> running risks which are too great.
> But, without "wish," "will" loses its
> life-blood, its viability, and tends
> to expire in self-contradiction. If
> you have only "will" and no "wish,"
> you have the dried-up Victorian, neo-
> puritan man. If you have only "wish"
> and no "will," you have the driven,
> unfree, infantile person who, as an
> adult-remaining-an-infant, may become
> the robot man. (1969, p. 218)

Perhaps what we have documented here is the
central place in our experience which willing plays.
We have distinguished willing from will-power,
discipline, willfulness, will-lessness, wishing, and

63

release and seen how the experience of willing can serve the integrating function proposed. We have had to resort more to theoreticians in this section since psychology has until recently ignored research on the experience of will but we have found much agreement among them. Of course, it is much more difficult to describe the constituents of an authentic experience such as willing, although we have achieved that somewhat, than it is to describe the pathological or inauthentic experiences related to the crisis of will. Let us start with a particular kind of pathology related to this crisis and see what might be revealed by the problems of will.

Psychotic Compulsion: A Factical Mode

In our discussion of will so far, we have not yet addressed the temporal although it should be obvious that will, like hope, is future-oriented and open-ended. One wills a certain future, takes a stand to what is perceived in the openness but, as in hope, one does not narrow it down to a very specific outcome. A willing student does not know in advance what will be required but stands ready to respond in ways that will bring about learning. This way of being toward the future also involves a way of being toward the past. We will now look at what happens when the peson is not able to move beyond the past but, as in schizophrenia and advanced drug and alcohol addiction, makes the past and body central. This time, however, the stuckness in the past has to do with a pathology of will rather than of hope. We will use as a model of this kind of pathology the example of psychotic compulsion described by von Gebsattel (1938/1958).

The diagnostic category used for this particular patient is a European one, "anankastic psychopath." As clarified in a footnote (p. 172), the term "anankastic" is loosely defined as obsessive-compulsive and the term psychopath "refers to constitutional psychopathological elements in such patients" (p. 172). We have used the term "psychotic compulsive" in the heading since that term might be more familiar to American readers. Von Gebsattel describes this syndrome in this way: "The anankastic psychopath represents that kind of compulsion in whom the compulsive phenomena attain the most far-reaching systematic development" (p. 172). He goes on to describe, for this particular patient, how

64

compulsions rule his life, how he is never free of compulsions, from getting up in the morning throughout his whole day. What these compulsions mean concretely is "the incapacity to turn to the tasks of the day - e.g., school work - and to move further into daily activities and toward new goals" (p. 176). In line with our contention above that this syndrome represents a case of making the past central, von Gebsattel states: "therewith is impeded the temporalization of life - 'Becoming' is blocked, and the past is fixated" (p. 176).

In a further description of this way of living time, von Gebsattel writes:

> The past must be dropped, like stool, and the healthy life which is directed toward the future - be it explicitly or in the general condition of being able - continually deposits the past, leaves it behind, thrusts it off, and cleanses itself from it. Not so in the compulsive; here the past does not take on the past perfect tense ("nailed to the past" says H.H. of himself): thus it cannot be eliminated and left behind, since this would call for the very condition of one's openness for the future. As something unfinished, it exerts pressure and makes demands on the anankastic as the future makes demands on the healthy person. Thus, the anankastic patient not only does not move from his position, but also is flooded over by the past. . . . (p. 178)

Here we see again pathology involving the emphasis on past as the central form of temporality. This particular form of pathology, as evidenced by the anal references, has to do with the issues of the second stage of development. We have also described it as a pathology of will; that is, this particular way of living the past excludes the possibility of authentic willing. Von Gebsattel notes this contrast in his description:

> In this setting it occurs to us that the healthy person reserves the

special exertion of his will to perfection for certain activities where "it matters." . . . In contrast to the healthy person, the compulsive makes just this Unimportant and Irrelevant the object of his will to accuracy. . . . For, in the strict sense of the term, the action of the healthy person, his daily toilet, breakfast, going out etc. is already something other than repetition because it never appears detached from the orientation toward the future. . . . (pp. 180-181)

As noted above, the living of the past as central is common to all pathology and we consider these modes as factical modes as in illness where, for the most part, something happens to the person to call his or her attention to body and past. In our developmental scheme, we would see compulsive psychosis as an elaboration of the fear-fantasy syndrome centered on the issue of willing; that is, underlying the paralysis of will is the ever-present fear or anxiety. However, the focus of this syndrome is on the will; we see it as a pathology of will, a factical mode.

We would distinguish this mode of existence from a compulsion neurosis although both have to do with the issue of will. The neurosis would be a fallen mode, centered on the present and the ego, as distinguished from the self. Let us turn to a description of two of these neurotic modes to see whether or not these understandings have some justification.

The Compulsive Character and the Impulsive Character: Two Fallen Modes

From descriptions of being willing and from reflection on our own experiences of it, we can see a certain harmony between ourselves and the object of our willing; that is, we see something as inviting, appealing and we respond by taking a positive stand toward this object. Of course, there are disharmonic moments in the process, resistances and so on, but we are speaking here of the moment one experiences oneself as willing. Usually one sees this only in retrospect; for, to be conscious of willing would

66

mean to be self-conscious and not willing at all. We simply see something as desirable and say, "I want to do that." We represent this harmony between the person and his or her world at that moment by the symbol (P ←→ W), the arrows representing the fact that there is consonance between the way the person is shaped by the world and the way the person shapes the world. It is a co-constitution which is experienced as smooth, agreeable. This is the existential mode, the self-mode, the future-oriented mode of willing as well as hoping and the other modes represented in the titles of these chapters.

With regard to the issue of hope, we have already depicted the paranoid character as one who tries to shape his or her world without being open or receptive to the shaping by that world (P ──→ W). For the issue of will, this mode of existence is represented by the compulsive character, a neurotic mode. The other way of living out the ego mode with regard to the issue of will is to refrain somewhat from shaping one's world and to allow oneself to be shaped by it without really taking a stand. We represent this mode by the symbol (W ──→ P) and see the impulsive character as an example of this mode with regard to the issue of willing. Let us begin with a description of the compulsive character and see what insights we can derive from understanding it as an ego mode, as a distortion of the experience of will in the broader framework we are proposing.

Shapiro (1965) describes three aspects of the obsessive-compulsive style: rigidity, the mode of activity and the distortion of the experience of autnomy, and the loss of reality. In line with what we have said above about the lack of openness and receptivity to the world and a shaping of the world in a particular way (P ──→ W), Shapiro states: "The most conspicuous characteristic of the obsessive-compulsive's attention is its intense, sharp focus. These people are not vague in their attention. They concentrate, and particularly do they concentrate on detail" (p. 27).

The sharp focus of attention we saw earlier was also characteristic of the paranoid character (P──→W) with regard to the issue of hope. However, here we see further the willfulness involved in the compulsive mode:

> In general, the obsessive-compulsive
> person will have some sharply defined
> interest and will stick to it; he
> will go after and get the facts - and
> will get them straight - but he will
> often miss those aspects of a
> situation that give it its flavor or
> its impact. Thus, these people often
> seem quite insensitive to the "tone"
> of social situations. (p. 28)

Shapiro notes that the mode of activity, the way
the person shapes his world is around the central
theme of trying, of effort and that this is a
distortion of the experience of autonomy:

> When the normal person says that he
> will try to do something, he means
> that he intends to do his best to do
> it, but the obsessive-compulsive
> person does not mean exactly that.
> When the obsessive-compulsive person
> says that he will try, he means, not
> necessarily that he intends to do it
> or do his best to do it, but that he
> intends to tax himself with the task,
> admonish himself to do it, and per-
> haps worry about it. (p. 32)

We have characterized this mode of existence as
a fallen mode, one in which the ego is central rather
than the self-world dialogue and in which the ego is
active more than receptive. Shapiro's comments seem
to bring this point out further: "If, in other
words, we choose to characterize the obsessive-
compulsive's activity as driven, then we must also
characterize him as the driver. He not only suffers
under the pressure of the deadline; he also sets it"
(pp. 34-35). And Shapiro seems to be in agreement
with us in seeing this mode as a problem of willing,
noting that the experience "reflects a remarkable
distortion of the normal function of will or volition" (p. 34). Incidentally, Arieti (1972) in The
Will to Be Human speaks of the obsessive-compulsive
style as a specific disorder of the will (p. 197).

Being cut off from the attraction of the world
which would energize the person in his or her
willingness means that the ego has to supply the
energy for itself and this is characteristic of the

68

obsessive-compulsive style.   Again,   quoting Shapiro (1965):

> Impulse,   in this order of things, is not   the initiator or the first stage of   willful directedness and   effort, but   its   enemy.   Thus,   for   these people,   impulse   or wish   is   only   a temptation   which   can corrupt   their determination,   interrupt their work, interfere   with what they   feel   they "should"   want   to   be   doing,   or otherwise   endanger   their   rigid directedness.   They are,   therefore, cut   off   from   the   sources   that normally   give   willful   effort   its direction. . . . (p. 37)

Under the theme,   loss of reality, Shapiro deals with   the   ambivalence   involved   in   this   form   of willfulness   as   contrasted   with   the   whole-hearted experience of authentic willing.   He notes that these people rarely ask the questions "Does it feel true?", or "Is it really so?" (p.   50),   but rather "Does   it fit?" (p.   51).   Their decisions are then accompanied by a lack of conviction:

> As far as conviction is concerned, he is   characterized symptomatically   by two   outstanding features: doubt and uncertainty,   on   the one   hand,   and dogma,   on the other.   Psychoanalysis has already dissolved this paradox by demonstrating   a   significant relationship between the two.   Dogma arises in order to overcome doubt and ambivalence   and   to   compensate   for them.   (p. 51)

So the compulsive,   in isolating him- or herself from the energy supplied by the situation, sets the ego up as   the   driver   of the self   and   things   and,   as   a result,   his   or   her   willing   is   characterized   by ambivalence and lack of conviction and can be   better called willfulness.

Having seen this mode as one in which the person attempts   to   structure   the   world   without   much receptivity   (P $\longrightarrow$ W),   let   us   now   turn   to   an apparently opposite mode (W $\longrightarrow$ P) in which the person

69

is more will-less. We say "apparently" because the opposite of something in human behavior usually means the other pole of the same dynamic; in this case, a distortion of the genuine experience of will. In fact, in the case of compulsive behavior, it turns out that the compulsive often makes the major decisions in life impulsively (W $\longrightarrow$ P), the other pole of the dynamic:

> It is often noticeable that, despite all the weighing of pros and cons that precedes the obsessive-compulsive's decision, the actual decision or the actual change will be made exceedingly abruptly. Despite the total length of time consumed, the decision itself will be quite attenuated as compared with the normal person's; it will be very much like a leap. He will finally say or feel something like, "What the hell!" or "I've got to do something!" and pick the next suit that the salesman offers or quickly sign the contract. Once the choice is made, these people will often regard it as a new directive, admitting no new evidence and preferring to feel that the situation no longer allows of modification. (Shapiro, 1965, p. 48)

As the other pole of this ego-centered dynamic, we will consider the impulsive character who, rather than overplaying the ego role, underplays it (W $\longrightarrow$ P). We also consider this mode an ego mode, the opposite pole of the same dynamic. Shapiro describes the lack of control in this way:

> The distinctive quality of this subjective experience revolves around an impairment of normal feelings of deliberateness and intention. It is manifested in the nature of the experience, for these people, of "impulse" or "irresistable impulse" and in the significance of "whim" in their mental lives. (pp. 134-135)

Without belaboring the point too much, we also want to justify considering the impulsive style as a problem of willing. Shapiro describes the actions of the impulsive person:

> It is an experience of an action, in other words, that does not feel completely deliberate or fully intended. Yet, these are not experiences of external compulsion or of submission to moral principle. . . . they are experiences of exceedingly abrupt, transient and partial wish, wish that is so attenuated as to be hardly comparable to the normal experience of wanting or deciding and so attenuated as to make possible or even plausible a plea of, "Guilty but without premeditation." (p. 136)

Arieti (1972) also describes the psychopath, a variant of the impulsive character, as being characterized by a specific disorder of the will. As he describes this disorder, he says, "Therefore, his will is not mature but is weak and diseased" (p. 203). Further, "If our interpretation is correct, they are not as capable of willing as normal people are" (p. 204).

What we have been claiming about all the pathological modes is that they are body-oriented and centered in the past. For the ego modes we have said that they are ego-oriented and centered in the present. Arieti confirms these two postulates for the ego mode of impulsivity when he says, "He [the psychopath] is too egocentric to be concerned with the problems of society; as a matter of fact, he ignores society" (p. 200), and "Future satisfaction of needs is something that he cannot understand and that has no emotional impact on him. He lives emotionally in the present and completely disregards tomorrow" (p. 198).

Everyday Willfulness and Wishing: Other Fallen Modes

According to our understanding of Heidegger's Care Structure, it is not only neurotics but all of us who participate, for the most part, in inauthentic or fallen modes. Coming from the science of psychology, we are attempting to delineate these modes more specifically. For the issue of hope, we have described the fear-fantasy syndrome as the every-day inauthentic mode. For the issue of will, we are suggesting the willfulness-wishing mode, with one pole always inviting the other. Perhaps the term "passive-aggressive" brings out this bipolar relationship best. What seem to be opposite terms are actually two poles of the same experience; the passivity or lack of will is accompanied by an aggression or willfulness. But we want to speak here of the more normal or everyday experience of this dynamic.

None of us can be authentically willing all the time. For the most part, our willing deteriorates into a fallen or ego mode. When we lose the openness and relaxation involved in willing, we often substitute willfulness for willing. Here we begin making resolutions and become harsh and violent with ourselves, trying to manufacture the energy instead of allowing it to come from the situation or the world. We force ourselves or, as we say, "psyche ourselves up," give ourselves pep talks in order to carry out our intentions. New Year's resolutions provide a good example of this behavior.

And, when it happens that the resolutions don't work, and they usually don't, we tend to become passive and to resort to wishing. When a person says that he or she wishes something would happen, we can feel the lack of will behind this statement. We even have a term, "wishy-washy" to describe the person at this moment of experience. We recognize that the foundation of wishing is fantasy just as the foundation of willfulness always implies a bodily rigidity which signifies fear. This rigidity can't be sustained so the person becomes, we might say, over-relaxed, not flexible but almost as in sleep. These bodily postures differ from the posture involved in willing which would mean having a backbone but being flexible as well; the analogy of a dance might represent this bodily stance well.

In describing these everyday fallen modes of willing, we are not proposing a new morality or saying that people shouldn't fall into these modes. We are merely being descriptive and affirming Heidegger's notion that inauthenticity is a constituent of human existence. We can become overly ambitious about this and strive to be authentically willing but the attempt to do so is itself

inauthentic. Traditional psychology usually suggests
ego tactics to overcome this syndrome and there is
probably some value to these tactics. However, one
cannot will to will anymore than one can will to
hope. The person always wills something beyond his
or her own subjectivity or it is not willing.
Perhaps the best that one can do with regard to this
issue is to recognize that one is being willful or
will-less and to stop doing that. When the space is
not being used up by these modes, one may find
oneself willing again.

Summary

We have been attempting, in this chapter, to
broaden the traditional psychoanalytic understanding
and Erikson's understanding of the issues of the
second year of life to one that is based on
Heidegger's Care Structure. Following Erikson's
lead, we have understood the crisis of this stage as
a crisis of willing and have seen the issues of this
stage as related to this experience. We have seen
how the experience of willing brings with it an
integration of the body, ego and self and also of the
self and the world. In willing, one's bodily stance
is in harmony with one's ego control, both centered
on the willing relationship between the self and what
invites the self to will it. We have seen that
willing is inclusive of the past and present but
centered on the future, on possibility. When one is
willing, one's past and present are not distracting
or impeding. Affirming the contributions of
psychoanalysis, we have seen that the person is
limited willingness; one is limited by one's bodily
experience of anality, one's history of autonomy and
other facticities of one's life. The person is also
habitually falling into the inauthentic modes of
willfulness and wishing and it is within this context
that willing takes place.

We have pointed to a representative form of
pathology related to the issue of willing, namely
compulsive psychosis, and noted the central place of
past and body in this factical mode. We have
suggested the neurotic modes of compulsivity and
impulsivity as the poles of an ego-centered dynamic,
a perversion of willing. Likewise, the everyday,
inauthentic modes of willfulness and wishing have
been seen as a more common form of fallen will. In
these above forms, the central emphasis is ego and

the temporality of the present.

Although willing may seen theoretically to be a separate issue, we have tried to show that it is related to the more basic issues of hoping and, in fact, is a further elaboration of these issues for a newer stage of development with more advanced issues of a physical, psychological and spiritual nature. The experiences of the first year of life are built upon in the second just as these experiences form the prototypes for later experiences of hoping and willing, presenting both difficulties and opportunities. The reader, by now, should be somewhat familiar with the overall framework. Let us proceed to Erikson's third crisis of development and see the extent to which this framework leads to a more accurate and integrated understanding of our developmental experience.

CHAPTER FOUR

IMAGINING

The term which Erikson uses for the strength or
virtue stemming from a resolution of the third stage
of development is "purpose." From the descriptions
of the issues of this stage, we feel justified in
using the terms "imagination," "imaginative
participation," "creativity" and "sense of purpose"
as synonyms. In fact, Erikson, in relating this
stage to the issue of identity, also uses the term
"imagining" when he says, "I am what I can imagine I
will be" (1968, p. 122). We see imagining as the
existential aspect of this stage, the one which
integrates the separate experiences of it and the one
which follows the experiences of hoping and willing
developmentally.

Before proceeding, however, there is an
important distinction to be made between the
experience of imagination and that of fantasy. Most
psychologists do not make this distinction and, as a
result, there is much confusion. We understand
imagining as the experience in which one forms an
image of the possible. In this experience one feels
drawn to the actualization of that possibility and,
in fact, the body is already being poised for that
possibility. There is no break with reality involved
and the experience is harmonic. Take the example of
a child trying to learn basketball. Before he or she
can learn to sink a basket, the act of sinking the
basket has to be imagined. As the child does imagine
this act, the body is already forming itself in a way
that makes the successful act possible. In this act
of imagination one pre-consciously feels animated,
activated and eager to follow through on the act.
The world is perceived as inviting and interesting.

In contrast to this experience, we have already
described fantasy as one which stems from fear and is
in the service of evasion. Fantasy, unless it
becomes integrated in the act of imagination, remains
a retreat from reality. The body is experienced as
passive rather than poised. Rather than being
invited into the world, there is even a re-entry
problem experienced as one ends the fantasy and comes
back to ordinary life. Here ordinary life presents
itself as a foreign kind of situation calling for
more coping than before the fantasy. This rupture

with ordinary life is not experienced in the act of imagination. In imagination one is shaped by ordinary reality and is also in the process of shaping and forming it in line with the image. Fantasy deals with the impossible and the autistic, whereas imagination deals with the possible and the artistic.

In making this contrast, again we don't want to be perceived as saying that people shouldn't fantasize. It is a given of human experience that we all do. However, it seems that some psychologists tend to idealize the experience of fantasy and confuse it with imagination. The work of imagination or creativity is to take the material of fantasy, to give it shape and to communicate it to others. Fantasy, itself, is private and communication is a problem with it. The relating of our dreams, daydreams and fantasies is usually interesting only to those who have another interest in hearing them, such as spouses, psychotherapists or researchers and, even with these people, communication is a problem. Something more is needed to make such communication more than a one-way street and it is here that imagination comes into the picture. The artist or writer gives shape or form to the fantasy material and makes it something more than a literal rendering of it.

Bruno Bettelheim (1977) would seem to be in agrement with these assertions when he writes:

> To a considerable degree, dreams are the result of inner pressures which have found no relief, of problems which beset a person to which he knows no solution and to which the dream finds none. The fairy tale does the opposite: it projects the relief of all pressures and not only offers ways to solve problems but promises that a "happy" solution will be found. (p. 36)

Here we see the dream or fantasy as an escape from pressure (fear) and as an uncreative response. The author of the fairy tale shapes the material of fantasy and communicates this difficult material to children in such a way that it invites them into life. The promise of a happy ending may not be realized in life but, without its inspiration, even partial satisfaction is not possible. It should also be noted that our imaginings are much more pedestrian and reality-oriented than the stories of a creative artist who deals more in the symbolic realm.

The contrast between fantasy and imagination would also seem to be borne out in this further description by Bettelheim (1977):

> . . . those who live completely in their fantasies are beset by compulsive ruminations which rotate eternally around some narrow, stereotypical topics. Far from having a rich fantasy life, such people are locked in, and they cannot break out of one anxious or wish-fulfilling daydream. But free-floating fantasy, which contains in imaginary form a wide variety of issues also encountered in reality, provides the ego with an abundance of material to work with. This rich and variegated fantasy life is provided to the child by fairy stories, which can help prevent his imagination from getting stuck within the narrow confines of a few anxious or wish-fulfilling daydreams circling around a few narrow preoccupations. (p. 119)

As stated above, we restrict the term imagination to the forming or shaping of fantasy or other experience in such a way that the person can communicate in either words or action.

Hopefully, this distinction is now clear and we can proceed to describe the various issues involved in this stage of development and see whether or not imaging is the most crucial issue and the one which serves as the integrating principle for these issues.

The Phallic Stage:
A Partial Description of Facticity

As was stated earlier, traditional psychoanalysis offers a description of the ways in

which our early experience, essentially bodily
experience, becomes part of our facticity and
determines (we would say, limits) later life. We
identify this as a partial description because there
are other aspects of our early experience not
included in these descriptions, even aspects of
bodily experience. If we take a typical description
of the phallic stage (Noyes and Kolb, 1958), we see
how even the bodily experience is narrowed down to
specific kinds of bodily experience:

> Similarly at about three years of age
> there appears another stage in the
> development of pleasurable interest
> with a shift of source from the anal
> to the genital region. This phase
> continues until about the seventh
> year. With the advent of this phase,
> there is a concern with the differ-
> ence between sexes and the size,
> presence or absence of the phallic
> organs. (p. 29)

Now, the importance of these experiences has
been documented by psychoanalysis and their impact on
later life demonstrated, although not as totally as
sometimes appears. But the narrowing down to
specific kinds of bodily experience necessarily
excludes others which also have an impact on later
life. For example, we have spoken of the importance
of the horizontal position for the first stage and
the importance of the stand-taking for the second
and have asserted that one's history with these
positions also has an impact on later life, becomes
part of one's facticity. Similarly, for the third
stage, we would broaden the emphasis on the phallic
stage and assert the rather obvious fact that
movement is the prototypical characteristic of the
child at this stage and that ways of moving are being
established for later years.

Erikson speaks of this movement in ways more in
keeping with a psychoanalytic approach but we would
also mean something broader than that:

> The ambulatory stage and that of
> infantile genitality add to the
> inventory of basic social modalities
> that of "making," first in the sense
> of "being on the make." There is no

> simpler, stronger word for it; it
> suggests pleasure in attack and
> conquest. In the boy, the emphasis
> remains on phallic-intrusive modes;
> in the girl it turns to modes of
> "catching" in more aggressive forms
> of snatching or in the milder form of
> making oneself attractive and
> endearing. (1963, p. 255)

Here, again, the emphasis is on a particular form of bodily movement; that is, those movements representative of the sexual and aggressive themes of psychoanalysis.

Without arguing against the ways in which these particular movements establish determinants for later life, we would attempt to broaden the understanding of these first movements. In addition to the individualized movements established in one's early biological experience, there are also cultural ways of moving which are embodied by members of a particular culture. These movements are traditional and are handed down from one generation to another, not consciously but in the usual course of things. I may get some feel for these ways if I try to imitate the movements and gestures of a person raised in India, for example. Just as learning the language of a culture gives a unique insight into that culture, so also does moving in its traditional ways. The freedom and inhibition of certain kinds of movements and, in general, the ways of carrying the body in different cultures have psychological consequences as well; they involve a whole world-view. These movements, whether inborn or learned, become part of one's facticity, become limits within which one may express one's possibilities. This is not to say that there aren't also individual differences within the same culture as, for instance, between a very active child and a docile one. Nor is it to deny that the movements, both expressive and inhibitory with regard to issues of the phallic stage, are also determinants. All of these set limits for the child's later experience and become aspects of one's bodily facticity. These factical aspects don't exist in isolation, obviously, but are the incarnated forms of ego, self and social modes as well.

Psychoanalysis, however, focuses on the specific forms of bodily facticity associated with sexual and aggressive themes. So, although we will later describe envy and jealousy as issues in this stage, psychoanalysis centers these issues on sexual themes exclusively. The Oedipus Complex becomes a central experience for this stage. As Noyes and Kolb (1958) describe it:

> Continuous throughout the phallic stage up to the fifth or sixth year there exists, according to the conception of Freud, a period of attraction to the parent of the opposite sex accompanied by jealousy and rivalrous hostility toward the parent of the same sex. . . . Normally this potentially pathogenic relation is resolved by the mechanisms of identification in which the boy identifies with his father and incorporates the father's goals and standards into his own pattern of behavior. Likewise, the girl identifies with her mother, advances toward a healthy emotional maturity and finds gratification and security in a feminine role. (pp. 29-30)

It should be clear that we are not criticizing these assertions as untrue but we are stating that they come from a particular perspective and, if we adopt that perspective, we also see them as true. The problem is that the perspective becomes totalized and everything else is included within that perspective. We want to affirm that, for the issues of the third stage, the sexual and aggressive themes are relevant and that one's history with these issues sets limits for further possibilities and kinds of movements. However, the person is not defined totally by these facticities or determinations. Rather, we have the broader notion of the person as limited possibility, as an embodied self in dialogue with the world and others. We have tried to broaden the psychoanalytic conception of the bodily facticities of this stage and to emphasize forms of facticity other than the sexual and aggressive ones. So we want to proceed to incorporate the psychoanalytic contributions regarding this stage into a broader framework. Erikson has already done much of this work by extending the bodily aspect to

the ego and the social aspects.   Let's see how this
is accomplished with the issues of the phallic stage.

Initiative vs Guilt
Erikson's Three-Pronged Approach

On the bodily level we have already noted at
this stage an energizing, a new sense of movement and
a more active sense of "going at the world."   Erikson
sees this also as a crisis of the ego as understood
psychoanalytically   and   he   calls   this   crisis
"initiative vs guilt":

> Initiative   adds   to   autonomy   the
> quality of undertaking, planning and
> "attacking"   a   task for the sake of
> being active and on the   move,   where
> before   self-will,   more   often   than
> not, inspired acts of defiance or, at
> any   rate,   protested   independence.
> (1963, p. 255)

We note here the joy in activity and movement
experienced by the child; the focus is not yet on the
task, a fourth-stage issue.

This   freedom   of movement is, of course, not
without its own problems, as Erikson points out:
"The danger of this stage is a sense of guilt over
the goals contemplated and the acts initiated   in
one's exuberant enjoyment of new locomotor and mental
power. . . . " (1963, p. 255).   What comes into play
here are the civilizing forces and the conflicts
which accompany them.   If healthy, these forces will
provide channels for movement and activity but there
will always be some conflict before such an outcome
is   achieved.   It   would   seem,   at this point in
history, that the romantic notion of allowing the
child complete freedom of movement with no attempt to
guide it has been rejected as a viable possibility.

Erikson   describes   some   of   the   energizing
movements which call for the civilizing influence:

> . . . initiative brings with it
> anticipatory rivalry with those who
> have   been there first and   may,
> therefore, occupy with their superior
> equipment   the   field   toward which
> one's   initiative   is   directed.

81

> Infantile jealousy and rivalry, those
> often embittered and yet essentially
> futile attempts at demarcating a
> sphere of unquestioned privilege, now
> come to a climax in a final contest
> for a favored position with the
> mother; the usual failure leads to
> resignation, guilt and anxiety.
> (1963, p. 256)

He goes on to describe the fantasies of power which
the child experiences at this stage and the "fear of
finding the (now energetically eroticized) genitals
harmed as a punishment for the fantasies attached to
this excitement" (p. 256).

The ego crisis for Erikson, then, is tied up in
this conflict between the child's own uncivilized
urges and the prohibitions on their satisfaction, as
represented by the super-ego. As he puts it, "the
child must turn from an exclusive pregenital
attachment to the slow process of becoming a parent,
a carrier of tradition" (p. 256). And, if there is
too much of a repression and inhibition of these
fantasies, the child may become over-civilized with
the following effect:

> The resulting self-righteousness -
> often the principal reward for
> goodness - can later be most
> intolerantly turned against others in
> the form of persistent moralistic
> surveillance, so that the prohibition
> rather than the guidance of
> initiative becomes the dominant
> endeavor. (p. 257)

Most of the above comments have to do with
extending the bodily insights of psychoanalysis to
the ego level. Erikson also extends them to the
social more directly, as he indicates the economic
institutions or occupational roles as the ones most
directly relevant to the crisis of this stage:

> He [the child] remains, of course,
> identified with the parent of the
> same sex, but for the present looks
> for opportunities where work-
> identification seems to promise a
> field of initiative without too much

infantile conflict or oedipal guilt and a more realistic identification based on a spirit of equality experienced in doing things together. . . . . Social institutions, therefore, offer children of this age an <u>economic ethos</u> in the form of ideal adults recognizable by their uniforms and their functions, and fascinating enough to replace, the heroes of picture book and fairy tale. (p. 258)

For the child, then, there is a promise that the libidinal energy or the broader sense of movement may find an outlet in the social arena, in the work world, where such energy will be rewarded and where the complicated issues within the family may be dealt with on a more objective basis. The sight of those in uniform (policemen, firemen, doctors, nurses, etc.) promises relief from the jealousies and rivalries within the family and the child may imagine himself or herself in these roles which invite to greater growth. As in most of his writing, Erikson fulfills his intention of integrating the body, the ego and the social, this time with regard to the issues of the third stage of development.

Direction: The Fallen Aspct

We are again using Erikson's term to describe the ego or fallen aspect of this stage. When we look for the proper role of the ego for this stage, we see that its appropriate role is one of directing the already energized body. Just as prediction is healthy and necessary for realistic hope and just as control is needed for genuine willing, so too, the guidance and direction of energy and movement is necessary for imagining. Remember, here, our definition of imagining which is the first step in action. If I can't imagine myself doing something, I can't do it; if I imagine myself doing something, I am already engaged in the process of doing it. For this imagining to take place, the ego must not be standing in the way but must be integrated in the process.

However, as we have seen with regard to hoping and willing, these processes don't happen automatically nor without difficulty. One may fall into habits which interfere with the process and these habits we identify as ego problems or fallenness. We will later describe these ego problems in detail as depression and hysteria or the milder forms of boredom and enthusiasm. These will be considered primarily as problems of imagination centered on the ego, but, considered from the bodily aspects, they are also problems of movement, of moving too slowly or too quickly. When the ego's directing of the energy is not in harmony with the imagined possibility, imagination deteriorates into an habitual boredom (P $\longrightarrow$ W) in which the ego becomes more than a director of energy or enthusiasm (W $\longrightarrow$ P) in which the energy is discharged without direction.

When we use the term "imagination," we are also speaking of creativity and the ego aspect might be more readily understood under the latter heading. The place of cognition, calculation and control is usually described as less than central to the creative process. Obviously, it is necessary to have these aspects present but, by themselves, they are not sufficient to account for creativity. The process of creativity involves more than intelligence. As we have seen, it is a question of movement or action as well. But neither is movement the central component of creativity. Rather, the movement and the intelligence are harmonized in a certain way under the more central experience of imagination or creativity. We can again summarize these points by means of a figure which contextualizes these various issues:

Figure 8. The third stage of development

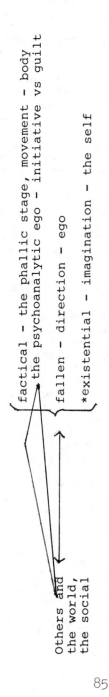

factical – the phallic stage, movement – body
the psychoanalytic ego – initiative vs guilt

fallen – direction – ego

*existential – imagination – the self

Others and
the world,
the social

85

In this figure, we see that the psychoanalytic description of the phallic stage comprises part of one's facticity. The bodily experience of the sexual and aggressive urges and the responses to them comprise part of one's history or facticity setting limits on the possibilities of imagining. The broader history of movement guided by one's culture and parents is also part of one's facticity. Erikson, represented by the triangle, brings out two other aspects for this stage, the ego crisis (psychoanalytically understood) of initiative vs guilt and the social, in this stage represented by the economic prototypes. We have added the ego aspect of direction to account for a broader range of behaviors also experienced in this stage and have suggested imagining as the existential aspect which contextualizes and harmonizes the other aspects. Thus, we see phallic issues, the issues of movement, initiative and ego direction as being gathered around the central theme of imagination, as being issues of imagination.

Imagination: The Existential Aspect

In hoping I open myself to the many perspectives of life; in willing, I take a stand in the face of this ambiguity; in imagining, I begin to move in certain directions. I imagine myself doing something and this image invites action which is smooth and integrated. Perhaps you have had the experience of passing many times something in your house in need of repair and have had the nagging feeling that something should be done to fix it. But the job seemed too complicated and one that called for many tools and materials. Every time you looked at it, there was a certain tightness felt and the exact way of proceeding was not clear. Then, it might have happened that one day, when you were relaxed, you looked at it a different way and a simple solution presented itself. Having imagined this solution, you were spontaneously moved to make the repair and spontaneously did so, later wondering why it became such a hassle. This, I think, is an example of an experience of imagination. Once you can imagine how to proceed, you are moved to do so. It is not a completely passive act but you have to imagine yourself doing it as well. Once the image is formed, action moves smoothly and the intelligence is enlisted. However, it is more than action and/or intelligence; the experience which integrates both is one of imagination. Here, we are not concerning ourselves with the skills involved in doing the repair, that is an issue of the next stage, but we are concerned with the opening of the possibility for doing the repair and imagination, like hoping and willing, is a future-oriented experience and one of possibility.

As noted in the beginning of this chapter, we distinguish the experience of imagination from that of fantasy. A fantasy doesn't invite the person's action and participation; in fact, there is the re-entry problem of waking from the fantasy. Imagination, however, invites the person and it has a different bodily feeling; the body is already poised to move toward the image in this experience. Unless this bodily component of the experience is present, it is not an experience of imagination but may be one of fantasy, wish or daydream. Another term which would bring out this aspect of the experience is imaginative participation. Imaginative participation would be distinguished from all forms of habitual participation, such as being bored, doing a routine job and so on. These latter kinds of experiences are fallen modes of imagination, ego problems. Yet, it is true that most of our participation is habitual rather than imaginative. But it is the initial imaginative act which calls us into action and sustains us.

Van Kaam uses the terms "originality" and "motivation" and they seem relevant here in fleshing out further the experience of imagination. In fact, motivation could be considered a synonym for imagination since it contains in it the notion of movement so central in the experience. Originality seems more related to facticity, the givens or ground for imagination and motivation. Van Kaam discusses the distinction between initial originality and historical originality; we would consider initial originality to be similar to imagination and historical originality to be similar to the factical basis for imagination. He says:

> A man's history thus has something to
> do with what his originality will be.
> We could call his originality, as it
> manifests itself at certain moments
> of his life, a historical originality,
> an originality which developed during
> his life history up to this moment.

Historical originality differs from initial originality. The latter is merely the possibility of being myself in a certain style which I receive as my birthright. In the beginning this gift is mere possibility. A person's history will tell what he does with it; whether he buries this gift or lets it come to life; how he develops his originality in response to challenges met by him. (1972, p. 2)

The historical originality is one's facticity with regard to the issues of imagination; the initial originality is the possible and more closely resembles imagination as we have been describing it. To be original is to be in consonance with one's facticity but something more is needed to activate this originality so that it becomes transformed into imaginative participation and van Kaam calls this "motivation":

My initial originality must be transformed into a concrete force that will shape my life realistically. I need an operational originality that becomes a driving power within me. What is that concrete guiding force? It is a fusion of many elements--an integration of guiding insight rooted in my experience of self and situation, of stimulating drive, of persistent effective embodiment of my will in concrete daily action. Have we a name for such an operational source of original action in man? We could call it "motivation." Not motive . . . Motivation is thus a fundamental enduring motive that has become an inner force that shapes my life continuously. (1972, pp. 4-5)

Perhaps it is clear enough from these statements what we mean by the existential aspect of this stage of development, the aspect of self, possibility and future. Motivation, a sense of purpose, imaginative participation and creativity are all used to describe

88

the experience which we have called "imagining." Of course, it is much more difficult to describe the open-ended experience of imagining than it is to depict the pathological, neurotic and everyday problems of imagination since they are closed and predictable. Let us look at these experiences which reveal the experience of imagination by what is missing in them.

Psychotic Depression: A Factical Mode

We have already described schizophrenia and advanced alcoholism and drug addiction as the factical modes of living out the issues of openness or hope. We have also described psychotic compulsion as a factical mode of living out the issues of will. We will now discuss psychotic depression as a factical mode of living out the issues of imagination or motivation. As you may remember, we are identifying these as pathological forms, as illness, in contrast to the neurotic or everyday modes. These modes center on past although present and future are lived out in deficient forms. They center on body although the ego and the self are also lived out in similarly deficient forms. The mode of psychotic depression is chosen as representative of a pathology of imagination. Mania or manic-depression would be other examples of this form of pathology.

We will, to start with, refer to Minkowski's description of a case of schizophrenic depression (1923/1958). The first thing to notice is the centering on the body. The patient Minkowski describes is a 66 year old man who felt guilty over not having become a French citizen and over his non-payment of taxes:

> An atrocious punishment awaited him as a result of his crimes. His family would have their arms and legs cut off and would then be exposed in some arid field. The same would happen to him; he would have a nail driven into his head and all sorts of garbage would be poured into his belly. . . Every leftover, all residue, would be put aside to be one day stuffed into his abdomen - and this, from all over the world. . . . All the matches, strings, bits of

> paper, and pieces of glass that he
> saw while walking in the street were
> meant for him. . . . Then it was
> rotten fruit and vegetables, cadavers
> of animals and men, the urine and
> faeces of horses. . . . And all this
> he would have to swallow. (pp. 127-
> 128)

This centering on body meant that his ego or the cognitive aspect of his life was wrapped up in bodily issues and his imagination became narrowed down to a few repetitive themes, more a description of fantasy than of imagination.

However, it is in the living of time that this factical mode becomes most clear. We may summarize this lived temporality as one that centers on a past full of guilt and fear of punishment, a present that is monotonous and repetitive and a future that is blocked. The other factical modes we have described also centered on the past but here the issues of this centering are the issues of the third stage of development, issues of imagination or movement. Minkowski describes the patient's experience of time in this way:

> Could we not, on the contrary,
> suppose that the more basic disorder
> is the distorted attitude toward the
> future whereas delusion is only one
> of its manifestations? . . .
> monotonously and uniformly, he
> experienced the days following one
> another; he knew that time was
> passing and, whimpering, complained
> that "one more day was gone" . . .
> However, our picture is still
> incomplete: an essential element is
> missing in it--the fact that the
> future was blocked by the certainty
> of a terrifying and destructive
> event. . . . In our patient, it was
> this propulsion toward the future
> which seemed to be totally lacking,
> leading as a result, to his general
> attitude. (pp. 132-133)

With regard to the living out of self or imagination, Minkowski describes what is present in

90

most people but missing in this patient:

> The personal impetus is a determining
> factor in more than just our attitude
> with regard to the future; it also
> rules over our relationship with our
> environment and thus participates in
> that picture which we have of that
> environment. In this personal
> impetus, there is an element of
> expansion; we go beyond the limits of
> our own ego and leave a personal
> imprint on the world about us,
> creating works which sever themselves
> from us to live their own lives.
> This accompanies a specific, positive
> feeling which we call contentment --
> that pleasure which accompanies every
> finished action or firm decision.
> (p. 134)

The imagining, which takes the body and past for
granted and which relies on the ego for the direction
of energy, results in completed actions which bring a
feeling of contentment. This experience of the self
in dialogue with the world is excluded because of the
centrality of body and past in this mode. This is
not to say that this patient never had an experience
of self or imaginatin but that the pathology
generally does not allow for such experiences.
Obviously, the self is there but in a deficient mode
as his future is blocked. Still, as Frankl
(1946/1971) asserts, the self mode is possible in
psychosis, but in a different way:

> The residue of freedom which is still
> present even in psychosis, in the
> patient's free attitude toward it,
> gives the patient the opportunity to
> realize attitudinal values. (pp.
> 161-162)

In our terms, we would say that one is still free on
the self level to assume different attitudes toward
one's facticity, toward one's pathology.

There are striking similarities between Frankl's
description of psychotic depression and Minkowski's,
with regard to the experience of body, ego and self
and with regard to the patient's living of past,

91

present and future. Frankl describes the bodily
experience, which is central, as a vital low
promoting on the ego level a big gap between the real
and the ideal accompanied by a falling away of the
self:

> What the vital low, the physiological
> basis of melancholia, produces is
> solely a feeling of insufficiency.
> But more than the physiological
> illness has come into play when this
> insufficiency is experienced as a
> feeling of inadequacy in the face of
> a task. . . . In the case of
> melancholia, psychophysical
> insufficiency is experienced in
> uniquely human fashion as tension
> between what the person is and what
> he ought to be. The melancholiac
> exaggerates the degree to which he as
> a person falls short of his ideal.
> (pp. 162-163)

And, with regard to the lived time of the
melancholiac, Frankl sees him as centering on a
guilty past with a falling away of the present and a
loss of the sense of aim in the future:

> When the underlying vital disturbance
> of melancholia increases the
> existential tension to an extreme
> degree, the person's life goal seems
> to him unattainable. Thus, he loses
> his sense of aim and end, his sense
> of future. "I lived my life
> backwards," a melancholiac woman
> remarked. "The present was done
> for--I lost myself in living
> backwards." This loss of a sense of
> the future, this experience of
> "futurelessness" is accompanied by a
> feeling that life is over with, that
> time has run out. (pp. 163-164)

In contrast to this pathological form of imagination, we might restate the ordinary experience of
these issues. I have a certain facticity stemming
from my experience of this stage of development,
highs and lows accompanied by certain evasive cognitions. I also find myself falling into habitual and

92

routine ways of participating and this is my usual
way. Despite this facticity and this fallenness, I
am able to imagine future possibilities which moti-
vate me to move forward. Or, another way of putting
it might be--it is because I have this certain facticity and own it that the possibility of imagining
opens up. It is because I become aware of my living
as habitual or routine that I am enabled to move
beyond this mode and to imagine a more promising
future. In psychotic depression, these possibilities
for imagining remain somehow latent. This is also
true for the neurotic forms of depression and hysteria and for the everyday inauthentic modes of boredom
and depression. The living of these modes prevents
the imaginative mode since I can't live both at the
same time. Let's look closer at these fallen modes,
these deficient ego modes which prevent and, at the
same time, form the groundwork for the experience of
imagination.

Hysterical Neurosis and Depressive Neurosis: Two Fallen Modes

Even though these are listed as two different
modes according to the predominant habituality, we
see them as opposite poles of the same dynamic, both
relevant to the experience of imagination. We see
hysterical neurosis as a case of the person being
habitually deficient in the shaping of the world
(W $\longrightarrow$ P) and depressive neurosis as an overly narrow
shaping of the world without the proper receptivity
(P $\longrightarrow$ W). In imaginative participation there is the
smooth, harmonic, dialogal experience in which the
person can be inspired to move and also shape the
movement (P $\longleftrightarrow$ W). Let us consider first the hysterical mode.

Here we will not attempt to give a complete
picture of this mode but will concentrate on those
aspects which inform the framework and are informed
by it. In terms of what we have said above about the
passive nature of this style, Shapiro (1965) would
seem to offer much confirmation:

> In intellectual matters, an
> impressionistic style--comprised of
> hunches and quick, relatively passive
> impressions--will tend to stop at the
> obvious, that which is easily and
> relatively immediately seen. The

second manifestation of this style of
cognition is impressionability. We
know hysterical people to be highly
suggestible--that is, easily
influenced by another's opinion; by
the pressure of real or imagined
external expectations; by fads,
current prejudices, and excitements;
and the like . . . A mode of
cognition or a type of awareness that
is characterized by the relative
absence of active, sharply focused
attention or by incapacity for
actively searching concentration. . .
. (pp. 114-115)

If we were to characerize the lived temporality
of this mode, we would describe it as a nostalgic
attitude toward the past, a sentimental one in the
present and an idealistic one toward the future.
Shapiro continues:

When we speak of hysterical
romanticism, we mean, I believe, not
merely time spent in romantic daydreams, but rather an outlook, a
romantic attitude, that permeates
everyday ideas and judgments.
Hysterical people, we know, are
inclined to a Prince-Charming-will-
come-and-everything-will-turn-out-
right view of life, to nostalgic and
idealized recollection of past
figures and place, and to a
sentimental view of the present.
(1965, p. 118)

We also postulate that the present is the
predominant temporality for these people. Acting on
present impressions and feelings, being carried by
the current fads and so on are characteristics which
probably come closest to Heidegger's (1927/1962)
description of Das Man or inauthenticity. Life is
lived as a series of unrelated "nows" as if the
present were the primary temporality. When one lives
the present as primary in this way, there is a
falling away of facticity and embodiment:

It seems that the hysteric's
romantic, fantastical, nonfactual and

94

> insubstantial experience of the world
> also extends to his experience of his
> own self. He does not feel like a
> very substantial human being with a
> real and factual history. (Shapiro,
> 1965, p. 120)

> But these patients seem to mean,
> further, "I dont' know what I am
> like." They seem to feel as if they
> were virtually weightless and
> floating, attracted here, repelled
> there, captivated first by this and
> then by that. (Shapiro, 1965, p.
> 121)

As we can also see from these quotes, the
future-orientation or integrative self-mode is not
much in evidence. It's as if in identifying oneself
with a changing, present-oriented ego, one excludes
the self, the self that can imagine the real
possibility. Shapiro (1965) speaks of the difference
betwen the self mode and the ego mode of hysteria in
this way:

> An emotion that emerges into
> consciousness as a result of a normal
> process of integration and
> associative connection of a half-
> formed and immediate impulse or
> feeling with existing interests or
> aims and other sentiments and
> tastes--such an emotion feels like
> one's own; it is consistent with
> one's self, and it feels deep. But
> this integrative development does not
> occur in hysterical people. . . . (p.
> 130)

In these quotes we also note the frequent references
to fantasy as opposed to imagination and we shall
return to this point in the next section.

In contrast to the hysterical mode, we have on
the opposite pole of this dynamic the depressive
mode. Here we are referring to neurotic depression
without the physiological basis noted in psychotic
depression. Many of the characteristics described
for the psychotic form are present here, too: the
guilt, the gap between the real and the ideal and so

on; however, the focus here is on the ego or the present more than on the body or the past. The neurotic depressive, like the paranoid and compulsive characters, narrows down his or her world and actively shapes it, ignoring those aspects which contradict the narrowness. Only here, because the crisis is one of movement and activity, the depressive is concerned with moving the world. As opposed to the lightness of the hysteric's experience of self and world, there is a heaviness experienced in the depressive mode. The depressive exaggerates his or her own role in moving things and in moving in the world. He or she identifies with this ego and loses sight of self and future. Rather than trusting in inspiration, as happens in the experience of imagination, the depressive feels that the ego has to be the source of all the energy and it is inadequate to the task of moving this heavy world. The future is seen as a repetition of this depressing present and, in this, we can see depressive neurosis, like the other syndromes discussed so far, as a failure or problem of imagination.

Everyday Boredom and Enthusiasm:
Other Fallen Modes

The dynamic we described above with the polarities of depression and hysteria can also be seen in the everyday, inauthentic experiences of boredom and enthusiasm. In fact, we can see boredom as a milder form of depression and enthusiasm as a milder form of hysteria. In doing so we are remaining faithful to Heidegger's view that so-called "normal" behavior is, for the most part, inauthentic. The ideal for a psycholoygy of the self is not normality; this is the ideal for an ego psychology. However, we would contend that the more normal or healthy the ego, the greater the basis for authentic (in this case, imaginative) action. Freedom from pathology opens up a greater possibility for authentic action but it is no guarantee. And there are also the cases where people have realized great possibilities despite the presence of pathology. Because the limits are more narrow, possibilities are fewer but they may still be realized. Too often traditional psycholgy has posed normality as the ideal without sufficient criticism of it.

Everyone has experienced boredom at one time or another; it is a normal experience. However, the experience shares with depressive neurosis the same distortion of time and the same mistaking of the ego for the self. Boredom is lived as an eternal present; if one were, as Becker (1973) describes, authentically facing the issue of death, then boredom would not be possible. In boredom, one experiences time as if one would live forever, as if one had too much time and this is an obvious distortion. There is a falling away of the awareness of past and future or, possibly, an identification of past and future with the boring present. In boredom one is not fully aware of the self-deception and distortion but it is there. The body is experienced as being out of harmony with one's action, usually as heavy and slow and the self or possibility is latent. That is one of the identifying characteristics of being bored; there is a lack of possibility and self-expression or expression of a value.

Enthusiasm is generally perceived as a normal, positive, healthy experience; however, if one gathers descriptions of the experience of being enthusiastic, a rather different picture emerges. Many of the themes mentioned in hysteria emerge and they are experienced similarly. In contast to the slow movement of boredom, there is quick and sudden movement in enthusiasm, often leading to accidents. A person is inspired, let's say, by an idea. He rushes to tell his friends about this idea and spends much time in trying to convince them of its worth. The speech is hurried and the person depends on his emotional conviction rather than on the worth of the idea in speaking to his friends. Often, the person is too excited and carried away to take the appropriate actions in communicating the idea; he can't sit still. There also tends to be something similar to a hangover once the enthusiasm has run its course. The enthusiasm may lead to a more imaginative participation but often, if it remains on the ego level, it returns to boredom from which it may have sprung. Excitement and boredom, highs and lows, and aesthetic attitudes often detract from the creative process rather than aiding it.

We can present the everyday inauthentic modes in a figure which may further bring out their inter-relationships.

Figure 9. Everyday inauthentic modes of the first three stages of development.

P → W		W → P	P ↔ W
fear	and	fantasy	a problem of hope
willfulness	"	wishing	" will
boredom	"	enthusiasm	" imagination

We have already noted the horizontal relationships of these three modes which exclude the authentic experiencing of the issues of the various stages. We might also discuss now the vertical. Here we can see fear or anxiety as providing the basis for willfulness and boredom. The narrowness of perception involved in fear and the rigidity involved in willfulness prepare one for the heaviness and restricted movement of boredom. We have also already mentioned the central place of fantasy in describing hysteria. We can also see how fantasy can provide the foundation for wishing and can lead to the unrealistic, wasted movements of enthusiasm. Developmentally, one builds upon the other. In the same way, we see the openness of hope providing a foundation for the experience of being willing, leading to imaginative participation in life.

We might notice here that the inauthentic modes described might be escribed as moods or feeling in contrast to hope, will and imagination which include feeling but are more than that. Later on, we will have more to say about moods but, for now, it might suffice to say that fear and fantasy are about the issue of hope, but mostly in the form of an evasion; willfulness and wishing are about the issue of will, but also mainly in the form of evasion and, finally, boredom and enthusiasm have to do with the issue of imagination, but again mainly in the form of an evasion.

Summary

In general we have been exploring the promise that the Care Structure of Heidegger may hold in both contextualizing and integrating the more specialized developmental insights of psychoanalytic, neo-psychoanalytic and traditional psychological approaches. We have been using the existential aspect in each stage as the integrating experience or principle for each stage of development. We have taken the general philosophical theme of existentiality presented by Heidegger and have, following Erikson, pointed to specific experiences which represent this theme and which can be empirically described.

For the third stage of development, "imagining" is the term we chose to represent the existential aspect. Our contention was that the various issues described by specialized psychological approaches for this stage could be contextualized and integrated when understood under the general heading of imagination. Imagining, like hoping and willing in the first two stages, is what we have described as the authentic experience of the issues of this stage. It was described as an experience of possibility, an experience of the authentic self, one in which the body, the ego and the self are experienced as harmonic, one in which the past, present and future are integrated, the primary emphasis being on one's becoming and, finally, as one in which the pathological, neurotic and inauthentic experiences may be understood more clearly.

First of all, we considerd the psychoanalytic description of the phallic stage of development under the general theme of imagination. We contextualized this description as a partial one, along with the factual history of one's movement, of the person's facticity; that is, as a description of the limits and determinations of a person's imaginings. Following Erikson's descriptions, we brought out the ego and the social dimensions of these issues, contextualizing them as such. So, in addition to one's facticity, we saw the crisis of initiative vs guilt as an ego crisis of this stage relating it to imagination and we also pointed to the social roles as outlets for the imaginative activity. We saw the task of the ego at this stage as one of directing the energy and movement, as being necessary to facilitate the imaginative or creative process.

We pointed to a pathology representative of the issues of this stage and described psychotic depression as a pathology or sickness of the imaginative activity. The descriptions given of this pathology seemed to support seeing it as being a centering on one's facticity, past and body. The neurotic modes of hysteria and depression were depicted as fallen modes of imagination, centering on ego and present and descriptions of these modes tended to support this understanding. Finally, the everyday, inauthentic dynamic of boredom and enthusiasm was also seen as a mode of fallenness, excluding the authentic experience of imaginative participation.

We concluded by bringing together the existential aspects of the first three stages and seeing them developmentally. The foundation for imagining was prepared for by hoping and willing even though these experiences are authentic in their own right. The person must be free enough of the fear-fantasy syndrome to open himself or herself to perceiving the invitational nature of the world and other people. In this openness, one must be free enough of the willfulness-wishing syndrome to take a stand toward what one perceives and to be willing to engage it. In the context of this openness and willingness, one must be free enough of the boredom-enthusiasm syndrome, the merely aesthetic mode, to imagine one's possibility for participation in it. The imagining always presupposs one's particular facticities or limitations and one's habitual living out of inauthentic modes. It is within the context of these two, also, that imagining takes place.

CHAPTER FIVE

COMPETENCE

This stage is generally understood as beginning at age five or six and lasting until the onset of puberty. As we have mentioned earlier though, chronological age does not absolutely determine the developmental stage. The determining factor is whether or not the child is devoting the greater part of energy to the issues of a present stage or, on the other hand, to the issues of an earlier stage. When the crisis of an earlier stage has been resolved to the extent that the child may leave it and move on to the issues of a current stage, we may say that the child has grown psychologically. We have also mentioned the risk involved in moving from one stage to another.

In this stage of development the child comes up against the resistance of the world to his imaginings or, as Erikson (1963) puts it, "the inorganic laws of the tool world" (p. 259). Imagination is not sufficient for the accomplishment of a task although it does go a long way in making it possible. I may imagine how I can make a repair in my house but I have not yet come up against the resistance of the world. Making the repair presupposes some physical, mechanical skill as well as the presence of tools. The child may imagine sinking a basket in a game of basketball but he or she has not yet performed this skillful action. The child may imagine making an ashtray out of clay but doesn't yet know of the properties of the clay which help and hinder the process nor of the technique which other people have discovered for accomplishing this task.

The issues involved in this stage we have gathered under Erikson's term "competence," or better, "a sense of competence." Let us again turn first to the psychoanalytic version of this stage, understanding it as a description of the bodily facticity associated with a sense of competence and the issues involved in it.

The Latency Period: Partial Facticity

Many psychoanalytic theorists would not consider the latency period as a stage at all. In many ways it represents a continuation of the issues of the phallic stage, but with much less intensity. As Noyes and Kolb (1958) describe it:

> From about the sixth year until the eleventh of twelfth year there is a relative decrease in sex interest. This is known as the latency period. While sex interests and activities do not disappear there are no such marked and significant psychosexual changes as are seen in both the preceding and following periods. (p. 31)

If the child is devoting the greater part of his or her energy to the issues of the phallic stage, there would not be a freedom to learn the social ways the elders are ready to teach. To leave those issues behind, at least enough so that the child can become interested in learning, is to begin to confront the issues of this stage of development.

According to this view, the resolution of the Oedipus complex consisted of identifying with the parent of the same sex and such identification continues and becomes more specialized during this stage:

> The child does, however, identify more strongly than before with the parent of the same sex and begins more differentiation along masculine and feminine lines. At this time it is important that there be close association with a parent or some other satisfactory person of the same sex with whom the child may identify in establishing masculinity and femininity. (Noyes & Kolb, 1958, p. 31)

Here we see a further aspect of facticity highlighted in this stage and it is the facticity or limits of possibility due to one's masculinity and femininity. In our approach we would say that not all possibilities are open to the person. The factical aspect describes what those limits are. In this stage one's limits as male or female are important although there are many other facticities as well. Because psychoanalysis puts so much emphasis on bodily facticity, these limits may have been overstated. Erikson describes how the experience of space may differ in men and women (1968, pp. 261-294). We also know from our studies in phenomenology that, if the experience of space is different, the experience of time, body, others, and so on is also most likely to be different. So, as we have been doing throughout this work, we want to affirm the partial facticity described by psychoanalysis but also to broaden the notion of facticity and describe the person as factical possibility with a person's identity residing primarily in his or her possibility.

The Factical Body as Instrument

Just as the reclining position represented on a bodily level the issues of hope, the standing position those of will, and movement those of imagination, the image of the child's movement as skillful represents the issues of competence on the bodily level. Whether the child is guiding his or her movements according to the rules of play or busy trying to make something work or learning to read, he or she is at the world, coming up against the resistance of the world to imaginings and responding to this resistance with more or less skill. Although sinking a basket may have been imagined, it is found that something more is needed in order to make the ball go through the hoop. And there are adults and older children ready to teach the skills needed and to encourage the child to practice.

For many of the skills presupposed in imaginings, it becomes necessary to become familiar with tools: pencils for writing, hammers for building things, and so on. However, the most frequent tool and the most important basis for competence is one's own body. The limits of competence are already established by inherited intelligence, physical dexterity and, in general, physiological givens along with the embodiment of the cultural ways of doing things handed down from the past. Whereas, in the previous stage, the body was more involved by way of exuberance and joy in movement, in this stage the body is experienced as instrument, as refined and skillful movement. In games, the child comes up against rules and there are countless arguments about whether one did or did not step on the line, whether or not the rope touched one in jump rope or whether one was killed or only wounded by the imaginary bullet or ray from an imaginary gun. The body is not free to move in any way but in this specific way at this specific time.

Now, when we adopt the psychoanalytic perspective on the body, even in broadening it, we are not splitting the person into parts. Seeing the body as a central aspect of facticity does not mean that it is not operative in the fallen or existential modes as well. Obviously, in the fallen modes, the body is experienced as awkward and, in the existential modes, as harmonic with the self. We are making the body a central theme of facticity because it does set limits to one's possibilities. When we speak of the past as factical, this is also embodied. For this stage, the skills handed down by the culture begin to be embodied by the child. And, prior to this stage, cultural limitations are being set for the learning of some skills and not of others. However, contrary to psychoanalysis, we are not identifying the child with his or her embodiment as determined. For this stage the bodily and cultural determinations, including the sexual determinations outlined by psychoanalysis, set limits or boundaries for the realization of the possibility of competence, which is actually more a reflection of who one is than is facticity. As Erikson says of this stage, "I am what I can learn to make work" (1968, p. 127). Let us move on to Erikson's broadening of the psychoanalytical description with regard to this stage of development.

Industry vs Inferiority
Erikson's Three-Pronged Approach

In addition to what is occurring on the bodily level at this time, Erikson points to the ego crisis of industry vs inferiority and to the social task of entering into the technology of the culture. He emphasizes the shift from the "hothouse" of the family situation to the world outside the family and sounds close to our broader description of this stage:

> Thus the inner stage seems all set for "entrance into life," except that life must first be school life, whether school is field or jungle or classroom. The child must forget

106

past hopes and wishes, while his
exuberant imagination is tamed and
harnessed to the laws of impersonal
things--even the three R's. For,
before the child, psychologically
already a rudimentary parent, can
become a biological parent, he must
begin to be a worker and potential
provider. (1963, pp. 258-259)

Referring back to the resolution of the Oedipus
complex, Erikson emphasizes that the child must give
up the idea of becoming an immediate parent, must see
that there is no future for him within the family and
must begin identifying with the tool world. He
describes the ego crisis in this way:

He develops a sense of industry--
i.e., he adjusts himself to the
inorganic laws of the tool world. . .
. The child's danger, at this stage,
lies in a sense of inadequacy and
inferiority. If he despairs of his
tools and skills or of his status
among his tool partners, he may be
discouraged from identification with
them and with a section of the tool
world. To lose the hope of such
"industrial" association may pull him
back to the more isolated, less tool-
conscious familial rivalry of the
oedipal time. (1963, pp. 259-260)

We see here again in Erikson a most beautiful
integration of the bodily, ego and social aspects of
this stage. He names the educational institutions as
those which are most relevant to issues of this stage
and describes further the social aspect of the
latency period:

On the other hand, this is socially a
most decisive stage: since
industry involves doing things beside
and with others, a first sense of
division of labor and of differential
opportunity, that is, a sense of the
technological ethos of a culture,
develops at this time. (1963, p.
260)

107

He also points to the danger to the child and society when the child is not judged by what he can do but rather, as we would put it , on his facticity: "the color of his skin, the background of his parents, or the fashion of his clothes" (1963, p. 260). One cannot be responsible for one's facticity, only for actions within the realm of the ego or self modes. Erikson has already added much to the psychoanalytic description of this stage. Let us broaden it further by moving to a description of the fallen and existential aspects of this stage.

Method and Technique:
The Fallen Aspect

If we come to the more ordinary sense of ego and ask what its proper role is with regard to the issues of industry and competence, we see that method or technique provides a good answer. In order to be competent at something, the person has to learn the methods or techniques which will facilitate this competence. Even if one is not conscious of employing a technique, we can see that there is a way or method followed, that the person does a certain thing at a certain time in a certain way which facilitates the task. So we would say that method or technique is necessary for competence and that the proper function of the ego, the rational, controlling, calculative aspect of the person, is to execute this technique. There are some ways of doing things which are better than others.

This is so obvious in our time that to say it seems unnecessary; the greater problem is the reduction of competence to method or technique. In the popular culture and in the professional psychological culture, intimacy, friendship, love, and many other experiences have been reduced to "how-to" manuals, to a technical orientation. The problem, here, as mentioned before, is the absence of the existential aspect. When that is forgotten, then everything is reduced to an ego approach; in this case, competence is reduced to technique. We can see why, even though technique is essential to competence, the term "fallen" is most appropriate. Forgetting the broader meaning of competence, we "fall"into the habit of mistaking technique for it. In the technical approach we reduce everything to a matter of technique forgetting that someone can be technically excellent but a failure in the real

108

meaning of a task.

The fallen mode of technique is so prevalent in Western culture that it often takes the shock of another culture's approach to it to make it stand out for us. The problems described by a German philosopher in learning archery in Japan bring out the sorts of difficulties involved in mistaking the essential aspect of technique for the whole experience of competence. Herrigel (1953/1971) states what he has learned, first in a general way:

> One of the most significant features we notice in the practice of archery, and in fact of all the arts as they are studied in Japan and probably in other Far Eastern countries, is that they are not intended for utilitarian purposes only or for purely aesthetic enjoyments, but are meant to train the mind; indeed, to bring it into contact with ultimate reality. . . . If one really wishes to be master of an art, technical knowledge of it is not enough. One has to transcend technique so that the art becomes an "artless art" growing out of the Unconscious. (pp. v-vi)

In our terms, we would say that technique is necessary but that one must transcend technique in order to be competent.

This general statement, though, may not capture the power which the technical mode has over us. As Herrigel (1953/1971) describes his problems in letting go of it in learning archery, we can see ourselves in almost a comical way. He tenaciously sticks to a technical approach even while knowing it is ineffective:

> The strength needed for this unusual method of holding and drawing the bow caused my hands to start trembling after a few moments, and my breathng became more and more labored. Nor did this get any better during the weeks that followed. The drawing continued to be a difficult business,

and despite the most diligent practice refused to become "spiritual." To comfort myself, I hit upon the thought that there must be a trick somewhere which the Master for some reason would not divulge, and I staked my ambition on its discovery. Grimly set on my purpose, I continued practicing. . . . Though I breathed in technically the right way, whenever I tried to keep my arm and shoulder muscles relaxed while drawing the bow, the muscles of my legs stiffened all the more violently. . . . When, to excuse myself, I once remarked that I was conscientiously making an effort to keep relaxed, he (the Master) replied: "That's just the trouble, you make an effort to think about it. Concentrate entirely on your breathng as if you had nothing else to do!" It took me a considerable time before I succeeded in doing what the Master wanted. But--I succeeded. I learned to lose myself so effortlessly in the breathing that I sometimes had the feeling that I myself was not breathing but--strange as this may sound--being breathed. (pp. 21-25)

Here we see how the ego, rather than aiding in the process, may become an impediment and a hindrance to competence. The fact that most theoretical schemes include the ego but exclude the self is a reflection of the way in which we are gripped experientially in the fallen mode of technique.

In our approach, following Heidegger, we have been emphasizing the importance of time and timing. In fact, as we have already described for other stages, the ego modes are identified by poor timing and the self modes by good timing, by being in tune with lived time. In the next section, we will describe the experience of competence as one of good timing but the differences are very subtle. Perhaps Pirsig's (1974) description of the difference between an ego mode and a self mode in the experience of mountain-climbing may serve as a good transition point.

To the untrained eye ego-climbing and
selfless climbing may appear
identical. Both kinds of climbers
place one foot in front of the other.
Both breathe in and out at the same
rate. Both stop when tired. Both go
forward when rested. But what a
difference! The ego-climber is like
an instrument that's out of
adjustment. He puts his foot down an
instant too soon or too late. He's
likely to miss a beautiful passage of
sunlight through the trees. He goes
on when the sloppiness of his step
shows he's tired. He rests at odd
times. He looks up the trail trying
to see what's ahead even when he
knows what's ahead because he just
looked a second before. He goes too
fast or too slow for the conditions
and when he talks his talk is forever
about somewhere else, something else.
He's here but he's not here. He
rejects the here, is unhappy with it,
wants to be farther up the trail but
when he gets there will be just as
unhappy because then _it_ will be
"here." What he's looking for, what
he wants, is all around him. Every
steps's an effort, both physically
and spiritually, because he imagines
his goal to be external and distant.
(p. 206)

In reading these passages, one may be tempted,
because of our cultural confusion, to see the
solution in an anti-technical attitude. The opposite
of the technical attitude is the anti-technical
attitude and, in our view, these are merely opposite
poles of the same fallen dynamic. We will discuss
this dynamic in a later section of the chapter.

We may now summarize the broader view of this
stage of development in this figure.

111

Figure 10. The fourth stage of development

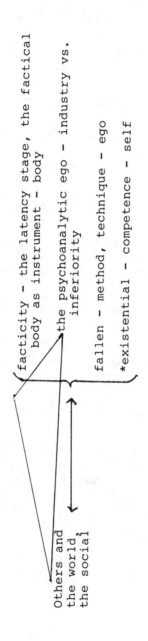

facticity – the latency stage, the factical
body as instrument – body

the psychoanalytic ego – industry vs.
inferiority

fallen – method, technique – ego

*existential – competence – self

Others and
the world
the social

112

Expressing these themes more explicitly, we may say that factically one's sexual history, the physiological givens and the experience of oneself as instrument set limits on the possibiities of competence. In addition, one is constantly falling into the habit of reducing competence to mere technique. Within these conditions, however, one does experience moments of competence in which there is self-expression in dialogue with the instrumental world. One may observe such moments in children who seem very much at home in their bodies when engaged in certain tasks. This at-homeness in the body is, of course, later disrutped by the onset of puberty.

Competence
The Existential Aspect

Competence, then, is the guiding theme which brings together and integrates the various issues of this stage: sexual identity as described by the psychoanalysts, the body as instrument, the issue of industry vs inferiority and the issue of technology. In the moment of competence one finds the resolution of these issues. The competence experienced does not have to be in an area adults take seriously; it may be in games as well. In fact, the experience of competence is most vividly seen in athletics. Every athlete knows the experience of being "hot" or being "on" when every movement is in synchronization with the rhythm of the game, when one "knows" where the boundary line is without looking, when it seems that one can see behind one, when one feels completely at home and in place on the playing field or court. Even the "high" described by long distance runners may be an example of this experience of competence. For most people, these are memorable moments in which they feel most alive and most themselves. Their bodies can be forgotten since they can be relied upon as instrument; they can also forget technique since that is also taken for granted; they experience, rather, a harmony between themselves and the task and this in an unselfconscious way.

Pirsig (1974), in the following conversation, describes less dramatically and perhaps more convincingly what happens in competence.

> Sometime look at a novice workman or a bad workman and compare his expression with that of a craftsman

113

whose work you know is excellent and
you'll see the difference. The
craftsman isn't ever following a
single line of instruction. He's
making decisions as he goes along.
For that reason he'll be absorbed and
attentive to what he's doing even
though he doesn't deliberately
contrive this. His motions and the
machine are in a kind of harmony. . .
. "Sounds like art," the instructor
says. "Well, it _is_ art," I say.
"This divorce of art from technology
is completely unnatural." (pp. 160-
161)

He uses the term "quality" where we might speak
of competence; his term emphasizes more the object
pole of the harmonic subject-object relation
experienced in competence. The experience of competence not only integrates the various aspects of
the person but also the self-world relation. Perhaps
that is what Pirsig means when he says:

Believe me, when the world is seen
not as a duality of mind and matter
but as a trinity of quality, mind and
matter, then the art of motorcycle
maintenance and the other arts take
on a dimension of meaning they never
had. (p. 240)

We have been calling this dimension the existential
one and, for the issues of this stage of development,
competence seems to describe well this dimension.

In each case (hope, will and imagination) we
have stressed the futural orientation as being the
most significant. For competence, too, this holds
true. The quotes from Pirsig given above already
hint at this fact but he makes it even more explicit
in the following. And, just as we have stressed that
hoping, willing and imagining have to do with the real
rather than the fantasized, he makes the point for
competence as well:

If you want to build a factory, or
fix a motorcycle, or set a nation
right without getting stuck, then
classical, structured dualistic

subject-object knowledge, although
necessary, is not enough. You have to
have some feeling for the quality of
the work. You have to have a sense
of what's good. That is what carries
you forward. This sense isn't just
something you're born with, although
you are born with it. It's also
something you can develop. It's not
just "intuition," not just
unexplainable "skill" or "talent."
It's the direct result of contact
with basic reality, Quality, which
dualistic reason has in the past
tended to conceal. (pp. 277-278)

Dualistic reason has influenced us to think that the
most real experiences of our lives, such as hoping,
willing, imagining and competence, are not as real as
the ones which can be measured and objectified. Yet,
for this stage of development, it is in the
experience of competence that one comes into contact
with the real, not the abstracted real of objective
consciousness but the real of human experience.

The Absence of the Factical Mode

No factical mode or pathology will be indicated
for the issues of this stage of development or the
following ones. Our contention would be that
pathology, at whatever age or stage it occurs, has to
do only with the issues of the first three stages.
Once the person has resolved the issues of hope, will
and imagination to the extent that he or she can
devote energy to the issues of later stages, then one
may experience the fallen modes of inauthentic
everyday behavior but these will be centered on the
ego and the present rather than on the body and the
past. Of course, the issues of this stage may prove
too much for the child or the adult and .there may be
a regression to the issues of the earlier stages. In
this case, pathology again becomes a possibility.
But the issues of competence and the issues of later
stages already assume a certain more or less healthy
resolution of the issues of the first three stages
and these issues are related to more advanced, less
primitive, themes. Let us move on to describe some
of the ego problems representative of the issues of
this stage of development.

The Inferiority Complex and the Superiority Complex:
Two Fallen Modes

    We are presented with a similar question with
regard to whether or not the ego problems of this
stage should be considered neurotic or merely
everyday ego problems. It is obvious that feelings
of inferiority and superiority are common and could
not be considered neurotic in themselves. However,
the question becomes more difficult when either of
these becomes so habitual that the person's ego
functioning could be described by these
typifications. These seem to be different enough
from the everyday modes of this stage to warrant
separate treatment but we would tend not to classify
them as neurotic modes. None of the fallen modes of
the later stages will be classified as neurotic
either because of the more advanced issues involved.

    Alfred Adler, who in his earlier work wrote much
about the inferiority complex, is not of much help on
this question because he presents a much more radical
and broad meaning of the term. In it he includes the
first stage issues of vulnerability, limitation (the
minus situation) and even, being-towards-death:

                To be a humn being means to have
                inferiority feelings. One recognizes
                one's own powerlessness in the face
                of nature. One sees death as the
                irrefutable consequence of existence.
                But in the mentally healthy person
                this inferiority feeling acts as a
                motive for productivity, as a motive
                for attempting to overcome obstacles,
                to maintain oneself in life. Only
                the oversized inferiority feeling,
                which is to be regarded as the
                outcome of a failure in upbringing,
                burdens the character with
                oversensitivity, leads to egotistical
                self-considerations and self-
                reflections, lays the foundation for
                neurosis with all its known symptoms
                which let life become a torture.
                (1933/1964, pp. 54-55)

We would agree with Adler that the basis of the
inferiority crisis is grounded in first stage issues
but would prefer to see the inferiority complex as a

more advanced form addressed primarily to the issues of competence rather than primarily to the fundamental issues of limitation, death and so on.

We would certainly not go so far as Adler (1929) in describing the seriousness of this problem. He writes:

> The abnormal feeling of inferiority has acquired the name of "inferiority complex." But complex is not the correct word for this feeling of inferiority that permeates the whole personality. It is more than a complex, it is almost a disease whose ravages vary under different conditions. (p. 74)

Here he seems to be identifying inferiority with what we have discussed in the first stage as basic anxiety or fear rather than limiting himself, as we do, to the habit of feeling inferior in the face of a task. The differences are due to a difference in paradigm.

Despite these differences, however, we also find some fundamental similarities. We have made the point that the seeming opposites in psychological functioning are often poles of the same dynamic. Adler (1929) presents this very clearly with regard to the inferiority and superiority complexes:

> Moreover, the two complexes are naturally related. We should not be astonished if in the cases where we see an inferiority complex we find a superiority complex more or less hidden. On the other hand, if we inquire into a superiority complex and study its continuity, we can always find a more or less hidden inferiority complex. We must bear in mind of course that the word complex as attached to inferiority and superiority merely represents an exaggerated condition of the sense of inferiority and the striving for superiority. If we look at things this way it takes away the apparent paradox of two contradictory tendencies, the inferiority complex

and the superiority complex, existing
in the same individual. For it is
obvious that as normal sentiments the
striving for superiority and the
feelings of inferiority are naturally
complementary. (pp. 78-79)

In our view, these modes which exaggerate one pole
over the other are attempts to avoid the ambiguity of
human existence. Rather than opening oneself to both
aspects of a situation, the person tries to eliminate
one. This maneuver narrows a person's life and, as
we have seen, always leads to problems as the other
pole presents itself. It is an essentially
uncreative approach to the ambiguity of life, cutting
off important sources of energy and opportunity.
Rather, it is the creative tension between both that
provides the grounds for authentic, integrated
behavior.

    We have described fallen modes as ego modes and
the inferiority complex as an ego mode centered on
the issues of competence. The child exaggerates the
place of his ego in the performance of a task, in
this case negatively. When the child comes up
against the resistance of the world to his
imaginings, he takes refuge in a negative ego mode
which diverts him from the task and the experience
of competence, of mutual dialogue between the self
and the task. Adler (1929) describes the cognition
which usually accompanies this evasion:

        The inferiority complex is often
        connected with the idea that a person
        has no special abilities. The
        opinion is that some persons are
        gifted and some are not. Such a view
        is itself an expression of an
        inferiority complex. According to
        Individual Psychology, "Everybody can
        accomplish everything," and it is a
        sign of an inferiority complex when a
        boy or a girl despairs of following
        this maxim and feels unable to
        accomplish his goal on the useful
        side of life. (p. 227)

Although we feel Adler overstates the positive ego
aspect in his maxim, we can see that the inferiority
complex is centrally a problem of ego. Whether a

person underestimates or overestimates his place in the process of competence, there is a centering on the ego rather than a centering on the task. The appropriate attitude in this process is one of humility, meaning that one evaluates one's strengths and weaknesses accurately.

Pirsig describes what happens when one exaggerates his abilities and speaks of this situation as the internal gumption trap of ego:

> If you have a high evaluation of yourself then your ability to recognize new facts is weakened. Your ego isolates you from the Quality reality. When the facts show that you've just goofed, you're not as likely to admit it. On any mechanical repair job ego comes in for rough treatment. . . . mechanics tend to be rather modest and quiet. There are exceptions, but generally if they're not quiet and modest at first, the work seems to make them that way. (1974, p. 308)

In summary, we feel justified in classifying the inferiority comlex and superiority complex as fallen modes centered on the issue of competence. We would not go so far as to label them or any of the later ego modes as neurotic because they have to do with more advanced issues. Both psychosis and neurosis seem to be related more to the issues of the first three stages. However, as fallen modes, we do see them as problems centered on the ego aspect, a falling into ego modes which detract from the possibility of the harmonic relationship between self and world experienced in competence. Let us now turn to a more familiar fallen mode, an ego mode centered on the exercise of technique.

The Everyday Technological and Anti-technological Approaches: Other Fallen Modes

With regard to the issues of competence, there is an everyday inauthentic mode consisting of two opposite attitudes which form a dynamic centered on the ego. We call these opposite poles the technological and anti-technological. Each pole

119

calls out the other and, as long as the debate remains on this ground, the issue of competence is never fully addressed. In fact, both attitudes are really evasions of the issue of competence; that is one reason for describing them as fallen.

The anti-technological pole is described by Pirsig (1974) as he sees it first exhibited in his friends' practice of having a competent mechanic take care of their motorcycle rather than keeping it tuned and adjusted themselves. He goes on to describe this attitude further:

> I might have thought this was just a peculiar attitude of theirs about motorcycles but discovered later that it extended to other things. . . . It's not the motorcycle maintenance, not the faucet. It's all of technology they can't take. . . . They talk once in a while in as few pained words as possible about "it" or "it all" as in the sentence, "There is just no escape from it." And if I asked, "From what?" the answer might be "The whole thing," or "The whole organized bit," or even "The system." . . . The "it" is a kind of force that gives rise to technology, something undefined, but inhuman, mechanical, lifeless, a blind monster, a death force. . . . Somewhere there are people who understand it and run it but those are the technologists, and they speak in inhuman language when describing what they do. It's all parts and relationships of unheard-of things that never make any sense no matter how often you hear about them. And their things, their monster keeps eating up land and polluting their air and lakes, and there is no way to strike back at it, and hardly any way to escape it. . . . So the final feeling is hostile, and I think that's ultimately what's involved with this otherwise unexplainable attitude of John and Sylvia. Anything to do with valves and shafts and

wrenches   is   a   part   of   <u>that</u>
dehumanized   world,   and   they   would
rather not think about it.   (pp. 14-
17)

    Pirsig himself sees their flight from and hatred
of technology as self-defeating but does not see much
promise in the technological attitude either.   He
describes the technologists themselves who performed
their   jobs like chimpanzees,   as though there were
nothing personal in it:

> But   the   bigget   clue   seemed   to   be
> their expressions. They were hard to
> explain.   Good-natured,   friendly,
> easygoing--and uninvolved. They were
> like spectators. . . . There was no
> identification with the job.   No
> saying "I am a mechanic." . . . In
> their own way they were achieving the
> same   thing   John   and   Sylvia   were,
> living with technology without really
> having anything to do with it, but
> their own selves were outside of it,
> detached,   removed.   They   were
> involved in it but not in such a way
> as to care. (p. 26)

In these final sentences we see the self excluded;
rather   than   competence   as   a   self-mode,   the
technologists are involved in an ego mode,   an
inauthentic way of being toward the issues of
competence.

    Pirsig goes on to describe how these attitudes
are really most fundamental, not minor. He sees that
his   friend's way of seeing things is coming from a
completely different and specialized dimension, a
different   vision   of   reality which   he   calls
"grooving."

> He will not or cannot believe there is
> anything in this world for which grooving
> is not the way to go. That's the dimension
> he's in.   The groovy dimension. . . .
> people in John's dimension are going to
> have to do more than just ignore it
> [scientific reality] if they want to hang
> on to their vision of reality. John will
> discover this if his points burn out.

That's why he got upset that day when he
couldn't get his engine started. It was
an <u>intrusion on his reality</u>. It just blew
a hole right through his whole groovy way
of looking at things and he would not face
up to it because it seemed to threaten his
whole life style. (pp. 53-54)

Pirsig describes the above style as romantic as
opposed to classical understanding and sees this
dichotomy as the source of the trouble:

Persons tend to think and feel
exclusively in one mode or the other
and in doing so tend to misunderstand
and underestimate what the other mode
is all about. But no one is willing
to give up the truth as he sees it,
and as far as I know, no one now
living has any real reconciliation of
these truths or modes. (pp. 67-68)

We believe that Pirsig's reference to Quality and our
own reference to the existential mode of competence
point in the right direction for such a
reconciliation.

We depict these two modes, the technological and
the anti-technological, as being the opposite poles
of a dynamic which is centered on the ego, the one
over-prizing its place in competence, the other
surrendering it. The problem is that, in this
dynamic, one cannot bypass the ego and move to the
world, that one does not allow the technique to
become part of oneself, that one cannot move past the
technique to an involvement of the self and the
world, the real self and the real world. This dynamic stands in the way of competence and prevents the
self-expression involved in competence and the expression of the object world as well.

A Review of the Inauthentic Modes in Dialogue
with Pirsig

We mentioned previously that the crises of the
various stages of development are not resolved once
and for all. Rather, when exposed to new
opportunities for growth, the earlier crises may
again return to be resolved in a new context. The
presence of fear and anxiety in adult life makes this

clear. Hopefully, we become better at recognizing these syndromes and at using prior experience as a guide to the re-resolution of them in new contexts. Pirsig describes the various traps into which one may fall in facing the issues of competence. They correspond well with what we have described as more fundamental issues.

When confronted with a problem of competence, one may return to a first stage syndrome which diverts one from the task at hand. Pirsig (1974) describes how this happens when one is stuck in not knowing how to remove a jammed screw in repairing a motorcycle. He says: "It's normal at this point for the fear-anger syndrome to take over and make you want to hammer on that side plate with a chisel, to pound it off with a sledge if necessary" (p. 273). The fear is in not knowing and, as we mentioned the traditional scientific method of prediction and control is of no use here.

> What you're up against is the great
> unknown, the void of all Western
> thought. You need some ideas, some
> hypotheses. Traditional scientific
> method, unfortunately, has never
> quite gotten around to saying exactly
> where to pick up more of these
> hypotheses. Traditional scientific
> method has always been at the very
> best, 20-20 hindsight. It's good for
> seeing where you've been. It's good
> for testing the truth of what you
> think you know, but it can't tell you
> where you ought to go, unless where
> you ought to go is a continuation of
> where you were going in the past.
> (p. 273)

In other words, the resolution of the fear does not reside in an ego mode but in a self mode and, in addition to the competence problem, the person has the older problem of dealing with the fear. We would say that the fear does not have to be faced directly as an issue here but may be resolved in passing as the issue of competence is resolved. If the fear becomes focal, the person is again dealing with a first stage issue rather than the more advanced issue of competence.

In facing the issues of this stage, one may also be diverted by a certain rigidity or willfulness.

> Of the value traps, the most widespread and pernicious is value rigidity. . . . This often shows up in premature diagnosis, when you're sure you know what the trouble is, and then when it isn't, you're stuck. Then you've got to find some new clues, but before you can find them you've got to clear your head of old opinions. If you're plagued with / value rigidity you can fail to see the real answer even when it's staring you right in the face because you can't see the new answer's importance. (1974, p. 304)

We see, here, that in facing an issue of competence, one may return to a certain willfulness, a second stage issue, which will impede the resolution of the dilemma. Depending on one's facticity in this regard and one's response to this facticity, one may spend more or less time on this more fundamental, but less task-relevant issue.

A third trap into which the person may fall with regard to competence is boredom, which Pirsig calls a gumption trap. "Boredom means you're off the Quality track, you're not seeing things freshly, you're lost your 'beginner's mind' and your motorcycle is in great danger" (1974, p. 310). The boredom trap is what we have designated as a third stage issue and it, too, may divert from the resolution of the fourth stage issue of competence.

So Pirsig gives us a feel for the actual dynamics invloved in this stage; he points out, especially, how the earlier stage issues may be involved. At this point, we can summarize the inauthentic modes adding to them the ones relevant to the fourth stage.

Figure 11. Everyday inauthentic modes of the first four stages of development.

P → W		W → P		P ↔ W
fear	and	fantasy	a problem of	hope
willfulness	"	wishing	"	will
boredom	"	enthusiasm	"	imagination
the technological mode	"	the anti-technological mode	"	competence

125

We would contend that the foundations of the technological mode reside in fear, willfulness and boredom
and that the foundations of the anti-technological
mode reside in fantasy, wish and enthusiasm. The
first set of experiences emphasize too much the activity of the ego; the second set are guided too much
by the power of the world. The technological mode,
also, we would assert, calls out the reaction of the
anti-technological mode.

It might seem from the above description that we
are proposing a compromise between the two modes, a
golden mean. On the contrary, if one tried to find a
mean between being too technological and not technological enough, one would still be straining to
resolve the problem on the ego level. Rather, we are
proposing that the mode of competence is different
from an ego mode, consisting of a different
experience of body, world, self and others. It transcends the ego mode and is primarily future-oriented.
The same holds true for hope, will and imagination.
They are not compromises but different modes of existence which we have named "authentic."

Summary

In this chapter we have attempted to arrive at a
more holistic, more integrated view of the psychology
of the fourth stage of life. We have tried to be
inclusive of the various contributions of specialized perspectives, identifying them as perspectives
and affirming what they have had to say as perspec-
tival. We have used Heidegger's Care Structure as
the integrating model and have pointed to the experiential base of the various aspects of the model. The
question of whether or not this is a true and useful
way of integrating these issues depends on the extent
to which it matches our experience.

The psychoanalytic description of the latency
period was included as an aspect of the child's
facticity with regard to the issues of this stage.
We expanded the factical aspect by adding to it the
theme of the factical body as instrument. Both
factical aspects provide the basis for and the limitations of one's competence. We then included
Erikson's description of this stage specifying the
ego crisis as one of initiative vs guilt, the bodily
aspect as the psychoanalytic depiction and the social
pole as emphasizing the technological ethos of the

culture. We then identified the more general ego aspect of this stage as one of method or technique and the integrating, existential aspect as one of competence. We asserted that the issues of this stage were not the central issues of any pathology or factical mode; they assumed enough freedom from pathology to have the energy needed to confront the issues. We did point to the two modes of inferiority and superiority as being representative of the inauthentic ways of being toward the issues of competence. We also pointed to the more ordinary, everyday inauthentic modes of the technological and the anti-technological and identified them as representative problems of competence. Competence was seen as being founded on hope, will and imagination and as sharing with them the integrating characteristic for their various stages.

Before moving to the issues of adolescence and early adulthood, we want to make a break in the format. Following Heidegger, we have been emphasizing the temporal aspect of human development. So far we have a fairly good picture of the past and the foundations for the issues of the next stage. However, since this stage is in between childhood and adulthood, we also want to have a picture of where these issues are heading. We want to consider adolescence and early adulthood not only in terms of the past but also in terms of the future directions. This will allow us to understand these issues from a broader temporal perspective. In order to carry out this intention, we will, in the next chapter, give a preliminary description of adulthood, not in its particular stages but in an overall way. The experience which seems to most accurately portray the experience of adulthood seems to us to be the experience of commitment. We will describe this experience and understand it as the one toward which the adolescent issues are pointing from the background of the earlier stages already indicated. In the later chapters we will consider the stages of adult life in greater detail.

CHAPTER SIX

ADULTHOOD AS COMMITMENT

The four stages discussed in previous chapters could be considered the foundations of an adult identity. Erikson presents them in this way and then goes on to develop his major contribution, the concept of the identity crisis and he describes it as a crisis of adolescence and young adulthood. Before discussing the identity crisis in our own terms, though, it seems important not only to know its past (the foundtions of the identity crisis) but also its future (the resolution of the identity crisis in adulthood). For this purpose, we will here present a preliminary chapter to a more informed discussion of the identity crisis.

In attempting a broad integration of the themes of human development, there is a danger of over-simplification. To say that the first four stages provide the foundations for identity, that the identity crisis follows and that adulthood is the resolution of the identity crisis seems a little too pat. One danger in this is seeing childhood merely as a preparation for adulthood rather than as an experience in itself. The other danger is to assume that one is finished with the issues of earlier stages once and for all. It is true that one's identity is founded on hope, will, imagination and competence but, at the same time, fear, stubbornness, enthusiasm and egoism are still operative and things remain complicated in experience. Still, there is a truth in the broad major themes as well as in the more specific and specialized ones.

In psychology until recently adulthood was hardly mentioned except as the period when test scores and measurements generally levelled off after reaching their peak. The impression given was that adulthood was a period of coasting, of greater and greater habituation and rigidity, a period of not much psychological interest. All this, of course, has changed and the depiction of adulthood has moved from one of stagnation to one of dynamism, including even stages of adulthood. We will consider the more specific stages later but at this point we will center on the experience of commitment as the central experience of adulthood and attempt to understand the identity crisis from this more futural perspective.

129

Description and Reflection on
the Experience of Commitment

In order to get some feel for the experience of
commitment and the structure involved, some years ago
I asked a graduate class to write out descriptions of
their own experiences of commitment. The class con-
tained a number of people returning to school after
other careers or raising families and the class members were older than average. What I am going to
present now are the themes and structure of that
experience as they described it. Although this study
was an informal one and not as precise as most
phenomenological research, the results have been
confirmed in other, more carefully structured
studies.

Most of the subjects described experiences of
commitment which had to do with marriage and work,
commitment to a person or to a life work. These are,
by far, the most common ones. However, there were
some unusual ones as well. One, by a retired U.S.
Marine colonel, was a description of his commitment
to a survival training exercise in which he volun-
teered to be dropped in the wilderness by parachute
and to survive on his own with a minimum of equip-
ment. Another unusual one was a description of a
commitment to owning a dog. Judging from the number
of stray dogs on college campuses, a number of
students in the identity stage were still experiment-
ing with that one.

With both of these and another I will mention I
had some reservations about whether or not these
experiences would have a similar structure to the
more ordinary descriptions by the others. Both,
however, turned out to be very similar to the others.
The one experience which ended up being very different in structure was a description of, in the subject's words, "The commitment to have an abortion."
This structure differed in tone and in substance from
the other ones, especially with regard to the good
feelings and integrity described by the other subjects. This subject discussed the written protocol
with me and was surprised herself to note the negative terms used in her own description. She gathered
other descriptions of the abortion experience and
obtained similar results. Still she persisted in her
view that it should have been a good experience even

though the descriptions made it evident that it was not. Because this protocol was so different, I did not include it in the study.

Results and Discussion

The first thing that strikes one about the descriptions is the paucity of information about the pre-commitment stage. There is little or no description of a struggle prior to the commitment, of the weighing of the pros and cons. Rather, the entry into the commitment is seen as <u>a response to an invitation</u>. From the vantage point of those who are committed, it seems as if the entry experience does not involve a strong intellectual component; rather, it is viewed as a harmonic situation of call and response. The call of the dog in the pet shop window and the response of eventually purchasing it gives a good feel for the tone of this initial stage. It may be that the view of the experience as one of rational decision-making, of weighing probabilities and of intense struggle may be a view peculiar to those who are uncommitted. There was no indication that the entry into the commitment was irrational, only that rationality was not central. On reflection, it would seem rather odd if one really were to choose a mate, for instance, on the basis of rational probabilities. Those who are constantly weighing the probabilities may be doing so precisely because they are uncommitted.

The descriptions given by the subjects begin with the more ordinary experience of being preoccupied with themselves and their own concerns and then being called out of that preoccupation by someone or something which draws their attention and <u>invites them into participation</u>. There is <u>a call of a situation; it calls one out of oneself and one's usual pre-occupations</u>. On reflection, we might understand the usual proccupations referred to as the calculative thinking of the ego mode, one's schedules, plans, routines and so on. Another way of stating this is to say that one is invited out of the inauthentic mode toward an authentic possibility, out of the fantasy of ego preoccupation into the shared reality of adulthood. In addition, it would seem essential based on these results that one experience the commitment as an invitation, as an opening up of possibilities, as futurally oriented. This stance wuld exclude coercion, a mere sense of duty and other stances opposed to the invitational; the absence of a sense of invitation means the absence of commitment as described here by subjects. All of the above descriptions may be considered as the first moment of the experience of commitment.

The second moment described is the response to the invitation; they simply make <u>a statement of the commitment</u>. Some described it as a <u>contract</u>, others as a <u>pledge</u>. In general, though, there is some <u>public declaration of the commitment</u>. There were also some feelings described at this point in the experience. The first was an <u>initial feeling of eagerness</u>; the second a <u>feeling that the commitment was irreversible</u>. Again, it would seem that these two feelings are essential to the experience. The feeling of eagerness would seem to flow from the invitational nature of the situation and its possibilities as discussed above. The awesome feeling that the commitment counts and is irreversible seems to be something that sets this experience apart from others. If the person, unlike these subjects, does not have the serious, even awesome feeling (some subjects called it "scary") that the commitment is a lasting one, it is questionable if one is really committed.

In fact, this may be the most important distinction between the identity crisis and adulthood. The identity crisis is about experimentation, trying this and trying that, but it's in the nature of experiments never to capture the experience. If a person experiments with commitment, some things may be learned but these things don't really reflect the experience of commitment. The essential structure is different. By its very nature commitment is not experimental; rather, it counts and this is a qualitatively different experience even if one goes through the very same motions. We don't expect children or even most young people to make commitments and don't hold them to their promises. There's some allowance in college, for example, for changing majors. However, at some point we do expect most people to make a free commitment, not under duress, and to make one which counts and lasts. If, at the moment of commitment, one feels that it is only a trial or an experiment, then the situation is so radically altered that it can no longer be called commitment. Often people can describe very vividly the radical way in which a situation is altered once the promise is made; the before and after is very striking.

Having responded to the call of the situation by making a commitment, one begins to realize that there is more to it than a statement. In the third moment subjects describe the ways in which the commitment mushroomed. They describe it as calling out for more than they thought it would. The tasks involved are more than predicted. In general, there seems to be an opening up of the commitment, a large number of specific tasks which follow from the commitment. It differs from the first moment in that one is called to perform specific tasks rather than merely to state the commitment; the brave words need to be followed by action.

A good example of the third moment for many people is the arrival of a new baby and the demands it makes on a couple. No matter how much experimentation is done and how much reading and advice given, one is never fully prepared for the experience. The calls are very specific ones and very simple ones, more humble perhaps than the noble words of the previous moment.

From reading the descriptions one gets the impression that subjects are pleased with themselves for having made the commitment and are experiencing the good feelings which come from the opening up of a new and promising future. Then they seem to be brought back quickly to very mundane tasks which call for their participation and, it seems, a large number of tasks leaving subjects with a feeling almost of being overwhelmed. However, the response to these calls appears to be smoothly made and one suspects that this relative ease stems from the fact that they are still in the honeymoon phase of the commitment, that the good feelings still carry them through these tasks.

In this moment subjects describe a deepening of the commitment through action. They express the realization that the commitment is open-ended, that it involves a history not just a moment. When these further calls presented themselves, some subjects made the interesting statement that they didn't understand the implications of the commitment at the time they made it. This statement is interesting in its ambivalence; it may indicate a true acceptance of the way things are and it may also provide a

133

rationale for the dropping of the commitment. There is a hint of regret here but, for most subjects, the challenge of these tasks is readily met. They speak of an increased awareness of implications and of the way in which the commitment grew in time.

The next moment, the fourth, consists of the expression of all kinds of positive feelings which followed from answering the calls of the third moment. In performing the tasks subjects describe an increased sense of purpose and meaning. They describe the nature of their involvement in these tasks as being intense and engrossed; they speak of a sense of personal involvement and even total involvement, of being wrapped up in the commitment. They describe a deepening of the commitment and an identification with it, one subject even declaring "I am the commitment." We can see here that the fulfillment of personal identity is found in committing oneself and that the answering of the calls of the commitment gives one one's identity. One subject, for example, described how she one day realized fully that she was a mother, this coming after four years of caring for her child. Up until then she had more of an abstact realization of that fact but it was only in living out the commitment that eventually she began to realize who she was. In the absence of commitment it would seem that one would have to remain in some kind of identity crisis or, at least, identity questioning.

The fifth moment in the experience again consists of further calls but of a more serious nature. By now it is becoming clearer to the researcher, and probably to the subject, that the structure of commitment is precisely this rhythm of call and response, a continual process of being called and of responding, a process which culminates in an adult sense of identity although that is not its purpose. The calls of this fifth moment, however, are not as easily handled as those of the third. The newness of the commitment having worn off, the consolations here seem to be few.

Subjects describe at this moment a real sense of personal struggle. The doubt that was only hinted at during the third moment becomes focal and they openly express doubt about the commitment; it becomes an open question of whether or not to continue the commitment. Some subjects express the doubt by saying they were not entirely rational when they made the commitment and at further moments of the commitment, that the process itself is not entirely rational. Here I think they are appealing to the prediction-control model of rationality prevalent in our society and correctly assessing that this experience does not fit it. The real question is whether this statement indicates an acceptance of the true situation or a rallying point for one's doubts and hesitations. It is obvious that the outcome is in doubt at this stage and that subjects are in a sober moment of the commitment, feel themselves at risk and are in a time of sacrifice and suffering.

As stated above, it appears that the structure of commitment involves this rhythm of being called and responding and that, at least at times, these calls are experienced as very harsh and demanding and one questions one's whole commitment or, in essence, the meaning of one's adult life. Apart from the obvious difficulties of the demands of adult life, what is it that makes this process so intense at times? According to the model proposed here, there is a crisis occurring in the experience of commitment. Up until adulthood the person has been developing a certain habitual mode, an ego mode, an inauthentic mode. How does one change or grow from this encapsulation? One of the primary ways is through commitment. What one is risking in the commitment is precisely the ego mode; for, one cannot retain it in its original form and still carry out the commitment. At moments such as this fifth moment of the experience, one is called upon to violate the assumptions and the habitualities of the ` ego mode. The commitment is calling for actions which are in contradiction to the habitual mode. Although many of the calls can be responded to without openly violating the habitual mode, some cannot. So it becomes a question of maintaining either the ego mode or the commitment at certain moments of the experience. The person may say, "I'm not that kind of person," the kind of person who responds in the committed way. If I'm a quiet person, the commitment may call for assertion. If I'm impulsive, it may call for patience and so on. This, I think, is the real struggle going on at these moments. The inauthentic self has been carefully nurtured; many defenses surround it; a whole system of rationalizations support it. To let go of it is a most threatening possibility; yet, that is what the commitment

requires at times. For the most part, we can avoid
this risk but at times, such as that of the mid-life
crisis, the choice has to be made. To the extent
that the ego mode can be transcended and the
commitment reaffirmed, to that extent one is able to
realize one's identity.

It also becomes clear that a commitment is not a
one-time affair.   One is actually participating in
the writing of one's adult history or the story of
one's adult life.   As with all the authentic
experiences, one does not arrive at a static state of
commitment but continues in the dynamic pattern of
call and response, of doubt and reaffirmation, an
ongoing process spiralling upward and/or becoming
stagnant.   Also, the process is never perfectly
lived out or realized.   People become more or less
authentic and, if they do become more authentic, it
is by modifying the inauthentic mode or habituality,
not by some denial of inauthenticity.

In the case of the subjects studied, they all
responded to the calls of the fifth moment by
remaining in the commitment.   Their comments of the
sixth moment, a moment of response, are sober and
heavy: "I overcame hardships I hadn't endured
before."   "I overcame doubt by putting one foot in
front of the other," and so on.   It is significant
that subjects are not taking full credit for their
response; it is not as if they are on top of the
situation. In fact, it seems as if they at times are
somewhat helpless to come up with the response on
their own but, instead, give themselves over to the
process, letting it work. One subject, for example,
talked about the experience of being carried along by
the commitment.   There is a humility involved here
which seems to have resulted from the experience.

At this moment, rather than making great claims
of achievement, subjects talk about their presence to
the situation in terms of being there and being
responsible.   The difficulties become apparent in
their   use   of   words,   such   as   self-
discipline, suffering and sacrifice.   One gets the
impression that the road was very difficult, that
they had been tested and had remained faithful.
Subjects give very simple descriptions of   the
feelings that accompanied their committed response to
these calls.   They express feelings of satisfaction
and worth, a feeling that the commitment was and is

worthwhile.   There is the presence of a stable   good
will and a <u>falling away of negative feelings</u>.

   Although subjects stopped here in the description
of commitment, they remained in those commitments.
So, the process of call and response, of doubt and
reaffirmation continues along with a growing sense of
identity.   This   process   we have characterized   as
adulthood   and   it   is   proposed   that   much   of   the
identity   crisis   has to do with the   envisioning   of
this future.   Before going into the identity   crisis
in   more detail,   let us see how others have reflectd
upon   the   experience   of commitment   and   attempt   to
arrive at a fuller description of adulthood.   In this
way I think it will be clearer what the issues of the
identity crisis are really about.

Other Reflections on
the Experience of Commitment

   Although there are few references in psychology
to the lived experience of commitment, Sidney Jourard
(1972), a humanistic psychologist, has at least
discussed the topic. The future orientation which we
have   found   characteristic   of   all   authentic
experiencing is evident in his definition:

> A commitment is my pledge to use my
> time   and   resources,   to   actualize
> someone's vision of a good or better
> world.   I   can only do what   I   deem
> worth doing, and so at any moment, I
> am   doing   those things,   to   produce
> that   future which I regard   as   most
> important, valuable and good. (p. 5)

   He   discusses   another central characteristic   of
commitment   which   we have also found,   the back   and
forth of call and response:

> I can see commitment as a response to
> the experience of a calling or   call.
> If   commitment   is a response   to   an
> invitation   or   a   call   to   regard
> something as important enough to drop
> other activities, then we can see how
> leaders,   teachers   and   prophets
> function.   Each   man   embodies   his
> commitments   and   lives   them   out
> through   his action.   Action   affects

137

the world. . . . (p. 6)

In addition to the call-response characteristic, the above quote also stresses the invitational nature of commitment, the absence of coercion mentioned previously. It also brings out the point that one is called out of the ordinary or habitual activities of life, that these have to be dropped. Finally, he brings out the point which has been stressed throughout this text, that ideals have to be embodied in order to be considered as something other than fantasties. These points are all consistent with the description outlined above.

It is to a philosopher we turn next for a reflection which both affirms and broadens the understanding of commitment described above. Westley (1972) develops further the meaning of promise as lived out in this experience. He begins by noting the contemporary ambiguity over the propriety of commitments, commenting that the jargon may be new but the fundamental ambivalence is not, "Man is both attracted to and repulsed by his commitments" (p. 10).

He distinguishes a promise from a contract by stressing the fact that a promise is a gift, "A Uni-lateral And Gratuitous Pledge Of My Person To Another" (p. 10). He goes on to say that "a man feels strapped by promises once the 'promise' has gone out of them" (p. 11). His characterization of promise or commitment captures the move from the identity crisis to adulthood:

> Promises are made because by making them a man puts himself into what he considers a "promising situation." . . . He commits his person in the joyful hope of bringing to actuality the promise which he foresees as possible in his life. (pp. 11-12)

We have noted in the earlier chapters the way in which neurotic and inauthentic modes tend to narrow down and specialize, avoiding the "both-and" quality of experience in favor of the "either-or." Westley points out two ways of doing this with regard to the experience of commitment:

> Those who dogmatically assert:
> "Promises must be kept," as well as
> those who while eschewing dogmatism
> absolutely proclaim: "Promises are
> dehumanizing and ought not to be
> made" effectively circumvent the
> basic ambiguity which we have found
> to lie at the heart of this problem.
> (1972, p. 12)

We will return to this point when we come to the
inauthentic modes characteristic of the identity
stage. It is enough to say here that dogmatism and
skepticism are indicative of this inauthenticity.

Westley goes on to discuss the problematics of
promising in more detail:

> The first group, let us call them
> A's, are those who give their word
> lightly and who do not seem to take
> promises too seriously. The second
> group, let us call them B's, are
> those who upon giving their word feel
> an inner compulsion to keep it -
> almost no matter what. . .. . This may
> not be, as so many B's like to think,
> the result of a moral superiority,
> but may only indicate that B's have a
> very great need for the respect and
> approbation of others, and keeping
> their word is one way to get it. . ..
> . B's accuse the A's of selfishness
> and insensitivity; and A's accuse the
> B's of inauthenticity and a lack of
> appreciation for the processional
> dimensions of human life. (pp. 15-
> 16)

He notes that one reason for so much
intellectual discussion concerning this topic is that
people are looking for reasons to justify what they
want to do, that "promising is not so much a matter
of reasons as a matter of will" (p. 19). In addition
to will, in the present model, hope, imagination and
competence are also involved in a foundatinal way and
none of these experiences fit the model of an
intellectual choice of a particular option on the
basis of probability. The most prevalent
psychological model is not an accurate reflection of

the way in which people live their experience. And so, we must go beyond modern psychology to learn abut these.

Erikson has suggested fidelity as the virtue connected with the resolution of the identity crisis. Fidelity is, of course, intimately tied up with the experience of commitment, as are the other adult virtues to be described. The relation of fidelity to promising and a preliminary glimpse of the virtue of fidelity is provided by Westley (1972) in his summary statement:

> To give up on one's promises because the promise has gone out of them is one thing: to theorize that promises are all without promise is quite another. The former posture, while regrettable, is understandable: the latter posture escapes all understanding. Those who aspire to fidelity, even after the original promise they sought goes out of the situation, remain faithful because their fidelity actualizes another kind of promise. They remain hopeful because they see some new promise in their fidelity, even after all other kinds of promise have vanished from it. Those who give up on their promises once the original promise is gone do so because they see nothing promising about fidelity under such circumstances. Each group does what it wants to. Ultimately, fidelity remains theoretically possible only for those more hopeful men who continue to see in fidelity a genuinely human response to life's promise. They are those among us who truly have the will to promise. (p. 20)

Summary

The identity crisis is at the center of Erikson's theory of development, the one we are using as a starting point for a broader understanding. Prior to a discussion of the identity crisis and the virtue of fidelity connected with it, we have paused to give a preliminary picture of the central issue of adulthood. This we have defined as the making and keeping of promises or commitments. Much of the struggle of the identity crisis can be related to the experience of commitment which, for us, signifies the ending of the identity crisis and the beginning of adulthood. Now that a preliminary understanding of adulthood has been presented, let us look more specifically at the identity stage in terms of the model we have proposed.

CHAPER SEVEN

FIDELITY

According to Erikson, fidelity is the virtue or
strength central to the issues of the identity
crisis. As is the case with all the virtues, the
possible is primary in this experience; one is not
actually faithful but is in the process of becoming
faithful. If the person were identified exclusively
with possibility, then we would find ourselves in a
position of idealism. However, Heidegger defines the
person as factical possibiity, as thrown possibility
and, because of this, we must first look at the
factical realm which opens up and sets the limits for
the possibility of fidelity.

The Beginnings of Genitality:
The Factical Aspect

As in the other stages of development, bodily
maturation makes for certain possibilities from which
the person was previously excluded. For example, the
capacity for standing up in the second stage makes
for certain possibilities of taking a stand not only
physically but psychologically, of being able to
will. In the same way with the onset of sexual
maturation, certain possibilities are opened up, new
issues are confronted and the fidelity we expect of
adults becomes a real possibility. Unlike
traditional psychoanalysis we do not identify the
person with his sexual history or even his bodily
history but with the way in which this history is
taken up. However, this history is an essential part
of a person's facticity and must be included in any
treatment of the realm of meaning or the realm of the
possible.

Noyes and Kolb (1958) describe this factical
aspect in the following way:

> Adolescence with its rapid
> physiological development of the sex
> organs and the maturation of sexual
> and reproductive capacities
> stimulates genital and heterosexual
> interests and activities. Sexuality
> is no longer diffused throughout the
> body as in the pregenital phases of
> personality development but becomes

focalized on the genital organs. (p. 31)

This change in the factical aspect alters radically the kinds of possibilities open to the person. Again, Noyes and Kolb (1958) point out and endorse the obvious one:

> Heterosexuality with its essence of love and the integration of its functioning into the purpose of mating, reproducing and the establishment of a family under conditions providing security and independence is a part of the individual's total development to maturity of personality. (p. 31)

To describe the factical aspect of this stage, not "genitality" but "the beginnings of genitality" was the term used because adult sexuality is not yet embodied at this stage. Although the biological possibility is there, the issues of the identity stage are not yet resolved enough for the person to be considered mature at this stage. Noyes and Kolb (1958) express similar reservations:

> By the time this stage is fully attained [the genital stage], a mature personality with a balanced structure of id, ego and superego should have been attained. Early adulthood is, however, with considerable individual variability, characterized by both maturity and immaturity of personality. Physical, physiological and intellectual maturity are already well established but patterns for the most efficient use of these aspects may not have been attained. In many individuals the maximum of psychological and social maturity of personality may not be reached for several years. (pp. 31-32)

In our own view the identity stage not only includes the working out of biological issues of earlier stages but also the psychological and existential ones, all this in the new light of the genital maturation mentioned above. So, again, the factical for the identity stage includes the beginnings of genitality rather than full-blown sexual maturity. The fallen aspects of earier stages are also involved as these habits of willfulness, inferiority etc. come up against the issue of commitment. Erikson adds to the perspective of traditional psychoanalysis many of these other issues as descriptive of the stage of development called "the identity crisis."

Identity vs Role Confusion: Erikson's Three-Pronged Approach

Erikson (1963), following the psychoanalytic emphasis, begins with the biological:

> But in puberty and adolescence all samenesses and continuities relied on earlier are more or less questioned again, because of a rapidity of body growth which equals that of early childhood and because of the new addition of genital maturity. (p. 261)

He then goes on to describe the ego aspect (ego as defined in psychoanalysis); he speaks of an integration taking place in the form of ego identity as "the accrued experience of the ego's ability to integrate all identifications with the vicissitudes of the libido, with the aptitudes developed out of endowment, and with the opportunities offered in social roles" (p. 261).

Even though the social aspect has already been included in the above descriptions, Erikson highlights the importance at this stage of ideology and aristocracy. As he puts it:

> In searching for the social values which guide identity, one therefore confronts the problems of ideology and aristocracy, both in the widest possible sense which connotes that within a defined world image and a predestined course of history, the best people will come to rule and rule develops the best in people. In order not to become cynically or apathetically lost, young people must

somehow be able to convince themselves that those who succeed in
their anticipated world thereby
shoulder the obligation of being the
best. (p. 263)

Erikson makes a big point of the prevalence of
ideology during this stage and of the ideological
mind. In the above quote he shows how ideology is so
necessary at this stage; the young person idealizes
those in the occupation desired out of a reaction
against cynicism. Ideology seems to be related to
adult work in much the same way as romantic love is
to adult love. In both, there is a distortion of the
true situation which seems necessary in our culture
as an entry into the adult experience. When the
ideological thinking extends into adulthood, as it
seems to do in the larger society, problems ensue.
It seems to indicate that the larger society is not
yet adult, clinging onto the ideological thinking of
adolescence. Thus, the dropping of ideology for many
becomes an individual task of the mid-life crisis
rather than a social affirmation of the true
situation.

Solzhenitsyn (1974), for example, makes a plea
for dropping the Marxist ideology but perhaps the
same case could be made for ideological thinking of
any kind:

To someone brought up on Marxism it
seems a terrifying step--suddenly to
start living without the familiar
Ideology. . . . The step seems a hard
one at first, but in fact, once you
have thrown off this rubbishy
Ideology of ours, you will quickly
sense a huge sense of relief. . . .
In our country today nothing con-
structive rests upon it; it is a
sham, cardboard, theatrical prop--
take it away and nothing will
collapse, nothing will even wobble.
(pp. 60-61)

In any case, Erikson's depiction of the identity
stage is well known. What we have attempted to show
here is the way in which he has extended the
biological emphasis (the beginnings of genitality) to
include the psychoanalytic ego aspect (identity) and

the social aspect (ideology and aristocracy). He indicates that fidelity is the virtue connected with the issues of this stage but does not develop it as another aspect. Before doing so, let us consider the fallen aspect of this stage and rather than using Erikson's term "devotion," we will speak of "constancy," a term which is somewhat overlapping.

Constancy: The Fallen Aspect

With regard to identity and fidelity there is a role for the ego, the ego as ordinarily understood, the strategic, functional aspect of the self. I can, by my own power and desire, make myself constant. I can show up on time; I can be steady and reliable and on schedule and so on and somehow approach being faithful but constancy also has its limits. It is to Marcel that we owe this distinction between the ego aspect of constancy and the self aspect of fidelity. Marcel (1964) seems very consistent with the model proposed here as he discusses the distinction: "First of all, it seems to me important to distinguish between constancy and fidelity. Constancy may be viewed as the rational skeleton of fidelity. It seems that constancy could be defined simply as perseverance in a certain goal" (p. 153).

As in the model proposed, in which the existential aspect includes and goes beyond the ego aspect, Marcel states:

> It may at once be observed, however, that constancy, construed as immutability, is not the only element entering into fidelity. Fidelity implies another factor which is far more difficult to grasp and which I shall call presence. . . . I am constant for myself, in my own regard, for my purpose--whereas I am present for the other, and more precisely: for thou. (1964, pp. 153-154)

When the ego aspect is harmonized within the existential as primary, then it has its proper place. However, when isolated from the existential, it becomes fallen, inauthentic. Marcel, in the same essay, describes constancy in isolation:

147

It should be noted that a being who is constant can make me see that he simply forces himself not to change, that he makes it a duty not to exhibit indifference on a certain occasion when he knows that I am counting on him. . . . I shall say of him that his behavior has been beyond reproach, that he has been absolutely correct; but how could this correctness of behavior be confused with fidelity strictly speaking? . . . However, I cannot with a clear conscience--without emptying my words of all meaning--say of him that he has been a faithful friend to me. (pp. 154-155)

There is something more to fidelity than mere constancy although constancy is an experience out of which fidelity may grow. Again, the lack of an adequate construct for the self in modern psychology leads to a confusion of the two. As in the other stage, the self mode or the existential aspect is what integrates the partial experiences and the issues mentioned so far in this stage. Fidelity brings together in a harmonic way the beginnings of genitality, the identity crisis of the psychoanalytic ego and the ordinary ego mode of constancy. Fidelity, in doing so, means then the end of the identity crisis and the beginning of adulthood. Repeated experiences of fidelity eventually bring about the resolution of the identity crisis.

We may outline the issues of this stage and fidelity's place in it in this way:

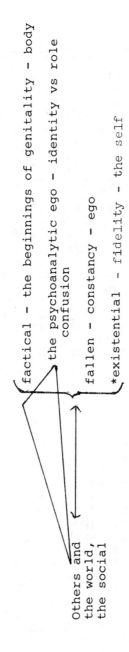

Figure 12. The fifth stage of development

factical – the beginnings of genitality – body

the psychoanalytic ego – identity vs role confusion

fallen – constancy – ego

*existential – fidelity – the self

Others and the world, the social

Let us now move on to a further description of fidelity.

Fidelity:
The Existential Aspect

We have already seen some hints of the structure of fidelity in the previous section. It is not merely an ego-driven constancy but a certain kind of personal presence, the object of whose concern is the other. Marcel adds to this description the element of spontaneity, an element which is reminiscent of the original invitation to commitment as described by our subjects when they discussed being called out of their usual preoccupations and attending to something or someone else. Marcel writes: "For fidelity as such can only be appreciated by the person to whom it is pledged if it offers an essential element of spontaneity, itself radically independent of the will" (1964, p. 155).

The mention of pledging in the above quotation reminds us that we cannot truly speak of fidelity without bringing in the notion of promise or commitment. The two are intricately tied up with one another. When we move from speaking theoretically to the experiential level, this relationship becomes even clearer. In giving an example of fidelity, Marcel necessarily brings in the experience of commitment:

> I am visiting an invalid; I come to see him out of pure politeness, perhaps; but I notice that my visit has given him more pleasure than I expected. . . . I commit myself to come to see him regularly. It is quite clear that when I make this promise to him, my mind definitely does not dwell on the fact that my present disposition is capable of changing. But let us assume that this thought does flash through my mind; I dismiss it, I have the feeling I should dismiss it and that it would really be an act of cowardice to take it into account. The moment I have committed myself, however, the situation is altered. Someone else has registered my

150

promise and henceforth counts on me.
And I know it. (1964, p. 159)

Here we have the first moment of commitment and also the experience of fidelity. The struggles and doubts of the identity crisis are brought together in this moment and also transcended. At certain points after the moment of commitment our subjects expressed the loaded idea that they did not know what they were doing when they made the commitment. This questioning is more typical of the identity stage and about this second-guessing Marcel has this to say:

> In short, how can I test the initial assurance which somehow is the ground of my fidelity? In principle, to commit myself I must first know myself; the fact is, however, that I really know myself only when I have committed myself. (1964, p. 163)

One is never absolutely certain about the commitment and the quest for certainty lands one back in the identity stage. The identity stage is one in which the young person is centrally concerned with the question of knowing the self. In our view, the question is never adequately answered and can't be, even partially, until the person makes a commitment and lives it out for a number of years. However, as with the progression from other stages, when the person's energy is devoted more to the commitment than to the identity issues of the previous stage, one could be said to be past the identity crisis.

The making of a commitment, however, is not enough; there is also the keeping of it. Of course, the virtue of fidelity comes in here. This is not to say that all commitments should be kept. For various reasons, especially at the point of making the commitment, it may be that it is not a valid one. The person in freedom may at some later point drop the commitment. When this happens, no matter what stage of the commitment the person has experienced, there is a going back to the pre-commitment phase. It is not as if the person can move laterally from stage three, say, of one commitment into stage three of another. Rather, one must again start from the beginning. People who move many times from one commitment to another reexperience the early stages of a commitment over again but do not experience the

151

possibilities involved in the later stages. As in the game of monopoloy, one goes back to "Go."

This paradoxical situation, however, of having to know oneself in order to be committed and of knowing oneself only through commitment reminds one of the young person's experience of looking for work. Experience is required but the only way of getting it is by obtaining a job in the first place. The paradox is built into the situation and traditional psychology has very little to offer for this situation because of its linear and specialized strategic thinking. One exception, however, is Gordon Allport (1962) who described commitment as the experience of being, "at one and the same time half-sure and whole-hearted." This expression seems to capture well the paradox involved and makes clear the fact that commitment is a matter of will as well as of the mind or perhaps more a matter of the will than of mind. Traditional psychology in general is more at home in intellectual calculations than in experiential descriptions. In the next section we shall use Allport's description of commitment as a basis for discovering the inauthentic modes of it.

Fanaticism and Faint-Heartedness: Two Fallen Modes

Beginning with the fourth stage, that of competency, the factical modes dropped out. A failure to resolve the issues of that stage and of the identity stage does not seem to entail fundamental psychological difficulty. Erikson does mention psychotic episodes at the identity stage but these seem to differ from the more foundational modes connected with the issues of the first three stages. At the identity stage and following it, it seems to be stretching things even to speak of neurotic behavior with regard to these themes. As a society, we may not even be beyond the adolescent stage; the prizing of experimentation and the ambivalence toward truly committed adults would seem to be evidence of this. However, the term "fallen" includes not only neurotic but also the more ordinary inauthentic forms of everyday life. So the fallen modes of this stage and the following come to appear as more and more "normal."

The two obvious ways in which people subvert the experience of commitment or fidelity are, to paraphrase Allport: <u>being full-sure and whole-hearted</u> and <u>being half-sure and half-hearted</u>. In these ways the fullness of the experience is reduced to a narrow specialization. The first mode, that of dogmatism or fanaticism, avoids the risk involved in commitment by fantasizing that one really has no doubts and that the commitment itself is an unqualified good. What makes the experience of commitment difficult is precisely the fact that one can never be totally sure; that's why it is only expected of adults. For many, because it is difficult to live in this ambiguity, the appeal of fanaticism is compelling.

If we think back to the subjects' descriptions of commitment, it is obvious that doubt is a recurring theme for them. In fact, another way of looking at its structure is as the back and forth between doubt and reaffirmation. This openness to doubt constantly brings the commitment into question, reminding one of limits, but also makes possible its dynamic quality and the strengthening reaffirmation. Also, without hope or openness, the foundatinal virtue, the later virtues cannot stand. Whether the young person commits in this inauthentic way to cults or lives this attitude in a more conservative-seeming situation, it is a fallen mode of fidelity, not an authentic form. If lived out habitually, one remains at the identity stage while appearing to be living out an adult commitment.

The other obvious way of handling the ambiguity of commitment and fidelity is to remain half-sure and half-hearted, even perhaps while engaging in seemingly adult pursuits. The attitude is that people change, things change and we don't know what's going to happen. So temporary and qualified commitments become the habit; there is an avoidance of whole-heartedness and willing. This attitude and mode also effectively circumvents the risk essential to commitment. However, to make an impulsive commitment would circumvent it as well. Rather, in the authentic experience, one is aware of the doubt but not paralyzed by it and, in making the commitment, expresses the self but, more importantly, the value of the person, group or work to which one is committed. To avoid the risk is also to avoid the fulfillment of one's identity.

Summary

This chapter has been concerned with the stage in between childhood and adulthood, in which the young person is bringing the issues of earlier development into integration with an imagined future of adult commitment. The bodily experience of sexual maturation, the growth in ego constancy and the new social themes of ideology and aristocracy bring to light newer issues for the young person. This is a stage of experimentation in preparation for the making of adult commitments. As Erikson notes, fidelity is tested in various ways during this stage as the young person comes to know himself/herself more and more. The questions of sexual identity, ego identity and constancy are the major ones and, at the appropriate time, are answered by the person's commitment and the fidelity to it. In this act, emphasis moves from the subject pole of identity to the object pole of the person(s), group and/or work to which the person is committed. The following chapters will describe this emphasis in more detail.

CHAPTER EIGHT

LOVING

Adulthood proper begins with the experience of commitment and the commitments made are usually, on the one hand, to persons and/or groups and, on the other, to projects. The two stages of adulthood being discussed here, loving and caring, could be considered to be dealing with the respective themes of love and work, the former more concerned with relationships, the latter with tasks. The former is being discussed in this chapter.

Erikson places the stage of intimacy before the stage of generativity and, in many ways, this placement makes sense. Especially from a biological perspective such as psychoanalysis, it makes sense that sexual intimacy would lead to the establishment of a family and children to be cared for and, therefore, that the stage of intimacy should be considered first. However, this kind of placement becomes less necessary the more one moves away from a biological perspective. In the current model, for example, career commitments could just as likely precede marriage and, in most cases, they do. So, even though the biological perspective of psychoanalysis is accepted in this model, the broader perspective of this model makes it less necessary to stick to a strict sequence with regard to these two stages.

However, as with the other stages covered, we do hold to a stricter interpretation of the sequence of identity and intimacy, as proposed by Erikson; that is, that the identity stage precedes the stage of intimacy. If it does not, it would appear to us that the person, even while appearing to be dealing with issues of intimacy, is doing so from a more central concern with identity issues.

Kilpatrick (1975) makes the same argument. He argues that essential to the experience of love is a strong conviction that it ought to last and that a stability of identity is a necessary prerequisite for love:

> . . . a constant love--one that does
> not alter with the passage of time--
> depends on an identity that does not

155

alter. In a sense, identity is an
even more "fundamental thing" than
love. It stands behind love. . . .
It is this persistent sense of
identity which allows us to make
brash declarations of friendship and
love such as, "You can count on me,"
or "Trust me." It is a confidence
that there is something durable about
"me," something that doesn't
fluctuate. Without that confidence
our commitments remain half-hearted.
. . . (pp. 1-2)

He also makes the point stated in the last
chapter that identity, in addition to being a
prerequisite for commitment, becomes fulfilled
through commitment:

Identity is also built on choices and
commitments. It is partly by
committing ourselves to others or to
causes or to passions that our self
develops. As identity develops, the
urge to share it grows more
insistent. Yet by giving ourselves
over to the things and people that
matter to us we get back a fuller
identity in return . . . we do, in
fact, identify ourselves by what we
choose to do and the people we choose
to be with. (p. 6)

Since most of this seems obvious, the
alternative may not seem apparent. Kilpatrick points
out that the concept of identity put forth by the
Human Potential Movement is one that violates the
sequence of identity and commitment. That movement
argues for a fluid self; one must flow with change
and with one's instinctual urges and avoid long-term
commitment. The emphasis is on the here-and-now and
it encourages self-actualization over commitment.
Kilpatrick sees this movement as only one of the
trends undermining the sense of a stable identity, an
identity which should culminate in commitment to
others.

In summary, throughout this volume we have been
adhering to the sequence of stages as proposed by
Erikson. Although there is some doubt about the

necessity of the intimacy stage preceding that of generativity, we hold firmly to the sequence of the identity stage preceding that of intimacy despite arguments made to the contrary. Likewise, we hold to the sequence proposed by Erikson for the earlier stages. Erikson's theory of development is the starting point and we want to be clear about any differences.

Intimacy vs Isolation:
Erikson's Three-Pronged Approach

Erikson makes the same point about this stage that he has made about earlier stages, the fact that one has to risk in the next stage what was so "vulnerably precious" in the last one. In this case, as soon as the young person develops a sense of identity, he or she risks losing it in involvements with others.

> Thus, the young adult, emerging from the search for and the insistence on identity, is eager and willing to fuse his identity with that of others. He is ready for intimacy, that is, the capacity to commit himself to concrete affiliations and partnerships and to develop the ethical strength to abide by such commitments, even though they may call for significant sacrifices and compromises. (1963, p. 263)

The fear of loss of identity, according to Erikson, may "lead to a deep sense of isolation and consequent self-absorption" (p. 264), and "The danger of this stage is isolation, that is the avoidance of contacts which commit to intimacy" (p. 266).

Unlike the other chapters, here we do not have a separate section on the psychoanalytic stage of genitality because Erikson covers it in his discussion of intimacy. In the previous chapter we indicated that the bodily aspect of the identity stage could be characterized as "the beginnings of genitality." At this stage and the following ones, the term "genitality" is used. Erikson says, "Strictly speaking, it is ony now that true genitality can fully develop" (p. 264).

While cautioning about the dangers of utopias, he does propose a utopia of genitality which includes:

1. mutuality of orgasm

2. with a loved partner

3. of the other sex

4. with whom one is able and willing to share a mutual trust

5. and with whom one is able and willing to regulate the cycles of:

   a. work

   b. procreation

   c. recreation

6. so as to secure to the offspring, too, all the stages of a satisfactory development. (p. 266)

Having discussed the biological pole of genitality and the ego pole of intimacy, Erikson also speaks of the social pole as that of ethics: "But as the areas of adult duty are delineated, and as the competitive encounter, and the sexual embrace, are differentiated, they eventually become subject to that ethical sense which is the mark of the adult" (p. 264). The closer one becomes to another person, the more danger there is of taking advantage and being taken advantage of. The ethical sense prevents such a situation from becoming habitual; this sense, according to Erikson, is different from the more passive morality of the child. Now one must participate in the discernment and decision-making about issues of involvement and it would be desirable if social guidelines and support were available for such ethics. As stated earlier, however, often they are not.

The Broader Model

At this point it might be well to situate Erikson's points for this stage within the broader model proposed and to outline the other aspects.

Figure 13. The sixth stage of development

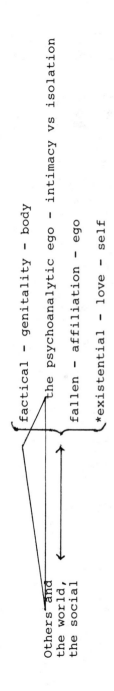

factical – genitality – body

the psychoanalytic ego – intimacy vs isolation

fallen – affiliation – ego

*existential – love – self

Others and
the world,
the social

159

What hasn't been mentioned so far is the fallen aspect and the existential aspect. If we ask what is within the ego control of the person at this stage, we come up with Erikson's term of affiliation. Although it is not true that we can force ourselves to love, we can on our own power affiliate with certain others. This affiliation may or may not result in committed love relationships. As Marcel has indicated, love as presence involves a radical spontaneity, something that is beyond mere willing. We have already indicated this as invitation and response and, of course, more than that is involved. In our day the term "love" has lost much of its meaning. In order not to add to that problem we will just say that it shares the structure of all the other experiences described as existential, although with regard to the issues of this stage: it is future-oriented and geared to the possibilities of the other; it integrates and harmonizes the issue of intimacy and the other aspects of this stage and so on. Also, since this model is not as biologically oriented, we include here commitment to groups and communities as well to the degree that people are committed to something other than their own needs and to the degree that their mission is positive and psychologically healthy.

In summary, it is in committing oneself to intimate relationships that new horizons open up for the young adult. In this continuing act one begins to harmonize the fact of being genitally oriented, the yearning for intimacy and the need for affiliation with the social opportunities. These loving relationships become one of the noteworthy aspects of one's adult life and are instrumental in the fulfillment of one's identity, although that is not their purpose.

Manipulation and Sentimentality: Two Fallen Modes

Two fallen modes which are related to the issues of this stage are manipulation and sentimentality. However, when we look at them more clearly, we discover that a more foundational virtue is also involved, that of will. Rollo May (1969) makes this relationship clear: "And will without love becomes manipulation--of which the age just preceding the First World War is replete with examples. Love without will in our own day becomes sentimental and

160

experimental" (p. 9).

In the above section it was mentioned that an ethical sense was necessary in love relationships because of the opportunity for damage. The closer one becomes to another person, the more vulnerable and defenseless one is. This is the capacity for abandonment, that one can let oneself go in these moments, that one can forget oneself and one's ego projects at least temporarily. With a strong or stable identity, one can allow oneself this forgetfulness because one is confident one will return to self-remembrance. The rhythm of forgetting oneself and remembering oneself is a characteristic of loving relationships.

However, there are these two ways of subverting the process. Rather than living in the ambiguity and many-sidedness of the loving experience, one may reduce it to an experience of willfulness or its seeming opposite, sentimentality. One may fall into the habit or ego mode of manipulation and avoid the risk and vulnerability of the experience of love. Of course, it takes two to carry off such a relationship and the other party would have to play a role of will-lessness in order to maintain it. As with all the fallen modes, the opposite involves similar dynamics.

Willfulness has already been described in Chapter Three; here, the willfulness involves the issue of relationship and love. Although willfulness is easily distinguished from love, it may not be as clear with sentimentality. Again, Rollo May (1969) is helpful in this clarification:

> This gives us, indeed requires of us, a clear distinction between care and sentimentality. Sentimentality is thinking about sentiment rather than genuinely experiencing the object of it. Tolstoy tells of the Russian ladies who cry at the theatre but are oblivious to their own coachmen sitting outside in the freezing cold. Sentimentality glories in the fact that I have this emotion. It begins subjectively and ends there. But care is always caring about something. We are caught up in our

161

experience of the objective thing or
event we care about. In care one
must by involvement with the
objective fact, do something about
the situation; one must make some
decisions. This is where care
brings love and will together. (p.
291)

Sentimentality can be recognized as being based
on fantasy, one of the basic fallen modes. As with
all the fallen modes, there is a duplicity involved.
One is able to maintain a picture of oneself as good
and noble without having to commit oneself in any
concrete way. When the sentimentality is lived out
in a committed relationship, there is bound to be a
challenge to it, possibly a crisis.

There has been much comment on this situation in
regard to the broader social context, the idea of two
different societal groups. There are the technicians
and the decision-makers who are schooled in
manipulation and the lethargic other group who, in a
will-less way, mutter about their self-actualization
and meeting their needs. Although this is a
caricature, there is some truth to the prevalence of
the habitual modes of manipulatioon and
sentimentality in our day.

Loneliness and Togetherness:
Two Other Fallen Modes

Two other modes, which have to do more centrally
with the stage of intimacy and love are loneliness
and togetherness, again two seeming opposites.
Rather than involving will, as do manipulation and
sentimentality, these two are more directly connected
with relationship.

To begin with, we want to distinguish loneliness
and togetherness from solitude and community. The
latter experiences are authentic and involve a
different dynamic. The experience of solitude is a
positive experience that refreshes and recreates the
person and, after a certain time, leads one back into
community. Likewise, the experience of community is
a positive one and involves the risk, vulnerability
and rewards of loving relationships.

However, such authentic relating cannot long be maintained and often degenerates into the habitual modes of loneliness and togetherness. These, too, operate in mutuality. In our large cities, for example, young people removed from any sense of tradition and community and living in isolated apartments, often live out this mode, if only because of the situation. As an escape from the individual loneliness, they may seek out crowds of people in a semblance of togetherness, such as is found in "singles bars." This kind of togetherness, rather than alleviating the loneliness, only seems to lead one back into it and this cycle is obviously distinct from that of solitude and community.

Although the pole of togetherness is involved in this dynamic, let us concentrate on the mode of loneliness and see more specifically what is involved. In doing so, we are preparing for a Heideggerian interpretation of moods and feelings and for a summary of all the fallen modes within a new framework. This framework will be presented in the next section.

For now, however, we want to understand more specifically what is involved in loneliness. To begin with, we are not talking about specific moments or temporary situations of loneliness, such as going off to college and so on. These are factical situations in which one finds oneself cut off from familiar people and surroundings and so forth. Everyone experiences this kind of loneliness once in a while. What we are talking about is the habitual state or mode of loneliness. The fallen modes we have been discussing are habitual modes, not merely factical situations.

Götz (1974) defines this kind of loneliness and offers some insights into its nature. He says:

> Loneliness is a <u>lasting feeling of distress or sadness caused by, or implied by, separation</u>, whether physical or mental, whether caused by others or inflicted by oneself upon oneself. It is important to realize that loneliness is a state, not the momentary pang or pain of separation. (p. 291)

He then goes on to discuss an often overlooked aspect of this mode in the traditional psychological treatment of feeling and emotion:

> But besides its characteristic as a state of feeling, loneliness involves a distinctive realization of one's willingness to entertain the mood, one's choice or acceptance of the feeling of grief and depression. This realization may be half-obscured and half-concealed; it may be buried under layers of rationalizations or seemingly honest queries. But it is there, and it is distinctive of the mood that is loneliness. Unless one is mentally sick, loneliness involves bad faith in the Sartrean sense, and like bad faith it is eventually evanescent. That is to say, the lonely knows "in his heart of hearts" (as the expression goes) that his grieving mood is not necessary, is not inevitable, and that therefore, if he persists in the mood and the mood persists in him, it is because he so chooses. (pp. 292-293)

In even stronger terms he says:

> The mood of loneliness is not forced upon me, nor am I compelled into it. It is a matter of my choosing to drink this brackish water, and of finding joy in sadness. Loneliness is a kind of masturbatory practice. As Fromm and Sartre have explained in different though related contexts, there is involved here a masochistic experience, and the lonely knows it. Only he can put an end to his self-inflicted misery. (p. 298)

We have described loneliness as being directly related to the themes of intimacy, relationship and love. It begins by being cut off from these experiences and it also ends by initiating these experiences:

164

> The answer to the experience of the interpersonal dimension of loneliness is fundamentally love. When you encounter this kind of loneliness you need someone to love, or someone who needs you, such as a member of your family, a lover, or a friend. (Sadler, 1974, p. 272)

However, because confusion and bad faith are essential constituents of the experience of loneliness, one does not move easily to love. For, the cognition most often accompanying the experience of loneliness is, "Nobody loves me." The person is somehow aware of the connection of loneliness and love but in such a way as to remain passive and lonely. What is obscured in this posture is the realization that could unlock the mood; that is, "I am not loving, I am not being a loving person." If one realized this fact openly, then one would be moved to reach out to others. With this schematic outline of the experience of loneliness in mind, let us move to Heidegger's interpretation of mood and see how all the fallen experiences mentioned may be more fully understood.

A Heideggerian Interpretation of Moods and Feelings:
A Summary of the Fallen Modes

Heidegger (1927/1962) refers to mood or feelings as "Being-attuned" and he sees moods as being much more capable of revealing a person's life situation than cognitions (pp. 172-173). In indicating this priority of mood over cognition Heidegger is very much in line with the modern age in which the expression "I feel" has replaced "I think." And every therapist is aware that the feelings of the client reveal a more fundamental attunement to the world than do his thoughts.

Heidegger (1927/1962) cautions, however, against surrendering science to "feeling" (p. 177) and he avoids the over-reverent attitude of moderns toward their feelings. He says, for example, "Factically, Dasein can, should and must, through knowledge and will, become master of its moods; in certain possible ways of existing, this may signify a priority of volition and cognition" (p. 175). Still, with these reservations, he sees mood as being capable of revealing much more than cognition or volition:

165

"Ontologically mood is a primordial kind of Being for Dasein, in which Dasein is disclosed to itself prior to all cognition and volition and beyond their range of disclosure" (p. 175).

What is it that moods can reveal? First of all, they can reveal the person's thrownness, the factical aspect of the person and the situation (p. 175). They can reveal the situation in which one finds oneself and which one did not choose. As Heidegger puts it, the moods reveal Dasein in its thrownness and "The expression 'thrownness' is meant to suggest the facticity of its being delivered over" (p. 174). Not only the factical aspect but the total situation of the person is revealed: The mood has already disclosed, in every case, Being-in-the-world as a whole, and makes it possible first of all to direct oneself towards something" (p. 176). So, if one interrogates the mood, it is possible to discover one's factical situation, both personally and socially, one's total situation and also to discover something that matters to us (p. 177) and toward which we can direct ourselves.

All of these revelations, however, are not that easy to come by, especially in bad moods in which "Dasein becomes blind to itself" (p. 175). There is also a seductiveness of mood which encourages this blindness. Heidegger often uses the term "evasion" to describe the way in which the person is toward his or her moods:

> In an ontico-existentiell sense, Dasein for the most part evades the Being which is disclosed in the mood. . . . The way in which the mood discloses is not one in which we look at thrownness, but one in which we turn towards or turn away. For the most part the mood does not turn towards the burdensome character of Dasein which is manifest in it. . . . Ontologically, we thus obtain as the first essential characteristic of states-of-mind that they disclose Dasein in its thrownness, and--proximally and for the most part--in the manner of an evasive turning-away.
> (P. 173-175)

166

And, finally, he says:

> A state-of-mind not only discloses
> Dasein in its thrownness and its
> submission to that world which is
> already disclosed with its own Being;
> it is itself the existential kind of
> Being in which Dasein constantly
> surrenders itself to the 'world' and
> lets the 'world' "matter" to it in
> such a way that Dasein evades its
> very self. (p. 178)

So, built into the experience of mood or feeling
is the evasion of what can be revealed through it.
What is evaded is the person's very self. For
example, the mood of loneliness reveals one's
isolation from others and one's life situation in
general as being cut off. At the same time it
reveals in such a way that the person evades. The
cognition "Nobody loves me" signifies the evasion.
Still, through the feeling of loneliness, one can
discover something that matters to one, such as the
fact that relationship and intimacy is at issue.
However, in evading, one maintains the ego mode of
loneliness and avoids the self mode of loving which
would be something toward which one could direct
oneself.

In a psychological sense all the fallen modes
which we have listed can be seen within this
interpretation and a summary of them could throw
further light on the dynamics involved. All of them
include the possibility of revelation but, at the
same time, all of them for the most part evade that
possibility.

In the fallen modes of fear and fantasy, it is
hope that is the possibility and hope that is being
evaded. The issue at stake is the issue of life and
death, the issue of meaning and the possibility is
openness and relaxation. One evades this possibility
in fear and in fantasy. In fear the possibility is
evaded by narrowing one's perception and being
hypnotized by one aspect of one's situation. In
fantasy the possibility is evaded by chemical "highs"
or everyday fantasy in which there appear to be no
limits to oneself or one's possibilities.
Maintaining the modes means maintaining the evasion;
confronting the modes means opening the possibility

of hope.

Compulsivity and impulsivity are two fallen modes in which the experience of willing, of taking a stand, of standing on one's own is being evaded. The narrow limits of compulsivity reduce life to a matter of control and the seductiveness of this mode is well-known. Impulsivity operates as if there were no limits and evades the possibility of a willingness within limits, the only kind appropriate to human beings.

In depression and hysteria the possibility of imaginative participation or sense of purpose is being evaded. Again, the singling out of one aspect of life, the burdensome, as a basis for one's activity is involved in depression and also in boredom. In boredom, the cognition "I am bored" evades the realization of the fact that I am boring and lack a sense of purpose in life. The unlimited activity of the hysteric and the enthusiast also keeps one from a realization of the true situation and one's possibilities in it.

Inferiority and superiority are two moods or modes of existence which evade the possibility of competence. Fanaticism and faint-heartedness evade the possibilities of promise and fidelity and, as we have just seen, loneliness and togetherness evade the possibility of being a loving human being.

Heidegger indicates that all these moods or modes reveal, if one chooses to look, the situation in which one finds oneself, the way in which it is lived, the issue that matters to one and the way that one could direct oneself to it. However, they also involve an evasion of these very possibilities, including that of being oneself. In the confused situation of contradictory psychological theories of emotion, Heidegger's position seems to provide a refreshing alternative, avoiding the over-reverence towards feeling or the overprizing of the cognitive aspect of the experience.

Summary

In this chapter we have discussed the first stage of adulthood proper although the order of the adult stages is not strictly endorsed. That is to say, experientially, the making of career commitments may just as easily precede the commitments to intimate relationships, the focus of this chapter. However, the case was made for the necessity for some kind of stable identity prior to the stage of intimacy, this sequence being affirmed. Erikson's aproach to this stage was broadened to include the existential aspect of loving in which one becomes oneself in the adult experience of making commitments to others. Manipulation and sentimentality, loneliness and togetherness were seen as ways of evading the possibilities of loving. Heidegger's interpretation of moods was presented as a way of understanding the evasion of possibilities in all of the fallen modes presented thus far. Now let us move to the second stage of adulthood in which one's promise is lived out in caring.

CHAPTER NINE

CARING

We have just discussed one major area within
which one may fulfill one's identity and that is the
area of human relationships. In committing oneself
to certain people, one is enabled to live out the
promise of one's adult life. As indicated earlier,
these kinds of commitments are reserved for adulthood
and for those who have sufficiently resolved the
identity crisis and those of earlier stages. Marriage is the most ordinary, but by no means the
exclusive, way in which this commitment is lived out.

The oher major way in which identity is
fulfilled is through commitment to a certain work or
project. The area of work offers the possibility of
fulfillment if one finds the kind of work or an
approach to work that makes it worth promising
oneself to it. Although, for most adults, the
ordinary sense of such fulfillment is a job or
career, for some, such as Gandhi, such work deserves
the title of mission. It should also be acknowledged
that the most humble type of work may be elevated to
the status of mission, as Gandhi and so many others
have demonstrated. Perhaps, as was stated earlier,
not many have achieved the state of adulthood; there
may be such a scarcity of adults that we see them as
exceptional cases.

However, another way of looking at adulthood is
from a more biological perspective. Here we see that
the children who were so anxious to grow up quickly
do so and become parents themselves. The work of
caring for these children is a task of adulthood and
one in which fulfillment is found. In fact, from
this perspective, one could consider that all work
which benefits future generations is adult work in
the true sense of the term. Erikson seems again an
excellent representative of this perspective as he
uses the term "generativity" to describe the stage
following that of intimacy.

<u>Generativity vs Stagnation:</u>
<u>Erikson's Three-Pronged Approach</u>

Generativity seems to be a good term to use for
this stage because it includes the biological fact of
having children, the generating or enlivening of

171

these children or others and the concern in general with the following generations. Erikson (1963) gives some feel for these different meanings in his definition of generativity: "Generativity . . . encompasses the evolutionary development which has made man the teaching and instituting as well as the learning animal" (p. 266).

In this statement we see generativity as having to do with the founding and carrying on of institutions, not only educational ones, but institutions, we might say, that incarnate values worth preserving. For example, legal institutions strive to keep alive the value of justice; medical institutions aim to preserve the value of care for the sick and so on. The task of keeping such institutions centered on the values for which they stand is a task of adulthood. When adults don't play their roles in this task, the institutions may produce the very opposite results: the letter of the law producing injustice, bureaucratic medical institutions not caring and so on. The adult missions of keeping the values alive are in conflict with such trends.

Erikson (1963) stresses that generativity helps to fulfill the adult as well as to meet the needs of the child: "Mature man needs to be needed, and maturity needs guidance as well as encouragement from what has been produced and must be taken care of" (pp. 266-267). We may think here not only of children but also of works or products, that, like children, lead us in certain directions and we follow their leads. In doing so, we fulfill ourselves without consciously setting this as a task.

Erikson goes on to extend the concept of generativity beyond that of generating children and shows how it is possible to be generative or adult without necessarily being parents.

> Generativity, then, is primarily the concern in establishing and guiding the next generation, although there are individuals who, through misfortune or because of special and genuine gifts in other directions, do not apply this drive to their own offspring. And, indeed, the concept generativity is meant to include such popular synonyms as productivity and creativity, which, however, cannot

replace it. (1963, p. 267)

We have already seen the social aspect of this stage in referring to the social institutions established and guided. It is not as if only the professions, for example, qualify as generative; rather it is every institution which represents not only a value worth preserving but a way of handing such values down to future generations. Erikson states it this way: "As to the institutions which safeguard and reinforce generativity, one can only say that all institutions codify the ethics of generative succession" (1963, p. 267). So, it is not the case that each generation has to reinvent the institutions which embody the values. They can inherit these although in this process they themselves are called to care or else these institutions and values become stagnant and even harmful. They may be called not only to accept but also to be critical or even to be founders of new institutions. As we have seen earlier, commitment is a dynamic, dialogal process in which doubt, uncertainty and struggle are involved.

The social aspect, however, is only one aspect. Erikson, as always, brings in the psychoanalytic ego and the biological:

> It has taken psychoanalysis some time to realize that the ability to lose oneself in the meeting of bodies and minds leads to a gradual expansion of ego-interests and to a libidinal investment in that which is being generated. Generativity thus is an essential stage on the psychosexual as well as on the psychosocial schedule. (p. 267)

And, again, he points out that, when the issues of one stage are not being faced, one falls back to the issues of the prior stage:

> Where such enrichment fails altogether, regression to an obsessive need for pseudo-intimacy takes place, often with a pervading sense of stagnation and impoverishment. Individuals, then, often begin to indulge themselves as if they were their

173

> own--or one another's--one and only
> child; and where conditions favor it,
> early invalidism, physical or psycho-
> logical, becomes the vehicle of self-
> concern. (p. 267)

From the above quotation one is moved to think not only of the retreat from issues of caring among married couples but also occupational groups. Profes- sional, for example, can become so stagnant with regard to the values involved that they become con- cerned primarily with their own benefits packages, professional bureaucracies and so on. There seems to be an unspoken agreement at times that such members will not challenge each other to meet the generative issue, the issue of caring, but rather that they will spend time protecting each other and nurturing each other. Such a generation, of course, does not pre- serve and hand down to the next generation the riches they have inherited from the previous, less selfish one.

The selfishness, self-preoccupation or narcis- sism of the current generation has been much discussed: the results of such a stance mean that one will also not reap the benefits of maturity. In discussing the experience of commitment, we saw that it was only after a period of faithfully responding to the calls of the commitment that one could attain to a firm identity within the commitment. Erikson makes the point that desiring to be committed is not the same as making a commitment and that more is required than the simple fact of undergoing it:

> The mere fact of having or even
> wanting children, however, does not
> "achieve" generativity. In fact,
> some young parents suffer, it seems,
> from the retardation of the ability
> to develop this stage. The reasons
> are often to be found in early
> childhood impressions: in excessive
> self-made personality; and finally
> (and here we return to the beginnings)
> in the lack of some faith, some
> "belief in the species," which would
> make a child appear to be a welcome
> trust of the community. (p. 267)

The parents' lack of faith is often reflected in the expressions of modern children. Despite the lack of material advantages children in traditional societies often appear happier and more hopeful than those of affluent modern ones. In any case, we have explored the three-pronged approach of Erikson and now seek to include it within our broader framework.

The Broader Model

Erikson's model has already included the bodily aspect of genitality, the psychoanalytic ego aspect of generativity and the social aspect of the societal institutions. For us, the genital stage is included as a partial characteristic of one's facticity; that is, for adult caring to take place, one's energies and investments must be capable of being centered on something or someone other than oneself. One must be somewhat free of sexual and personal neediness in order to care. Erikson has already described genitality in this way.

The term that we are using for the fallen or ego aspect of this stage is "production," a term also suggested by Erikson. In reference to care and the issues of this stage of development, there is a role for the ego as ordinarily understood. One can become productive on one's own power and will; however, one cannot care without first being invited to do so. If the production is within the mode of care, it is of a different quality than if it is production for ego gratification or external reward only.

We are now in a position to outline the issues of this stage within the broader model:

Figure 14. The seventh stage of development

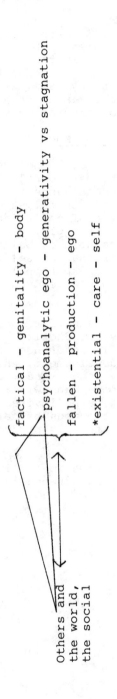

factical – genitality – body
psychoanalytic ego – generativity vs stagnation
fallen – production – ego
*existential – care – self

Others and
the world,
the social

As with the other stages, it is the existential aspect of care, in this case, which gathers up and integrates the other issues of this stage in a harmonic way. The integration takes place through caring action, the embodiment of values. We should make it clear that the care we are discussing here is the ontical, specific, lived experience rather than the broad ontological sense of care as in the Care Structure, the structure we are using to depict all the existential modes. Let us now take a closer look at the ontical experience of care.

Caring: The Integrating Experience

We have already identified loving and caring as the authentic experiences of adulthood, loving having more to do with issues of adult, intimate relationship and caring more with issues of responsibility for what has been generated, whether children, products, ideas and so on. The call to care as a central theme in one's life seems to be more connected with the time of middle adulthood.

So far, in the presentation of the existential modes of the various stages, we have stressed the foundational aspect; that is, that hope is the foundation for will and so forth. This way of looking at it has its own truth; for example, we quoted Rollo May as to the fact that love without will is not truly love. And we still hold to that foundational way of seeing these modes.

However, one further point which hasn't been clearly stressed is the fact that all the prior existential modes are involved in all the later ones in a newer way. For example, the issues of fear for the first stages may have been faced and more or less resolved, but then they may arise and have to be resolved in a new way when they take the form of a fear of intimacy, for example. The later issues throw the earlier resolutions into question and call for re-resolutions or new forms of resolution geared to the issues of the current stage. For example, although the hope of childhood and adulthood involve the same fundamental structure, there are also differences in how it is lived out. In general, the adult existential modes involve not only the resolution of current issues but also the re-resolution of earlier ones. Fortunately, we have a text, Mayeroff's On Caring (1971),which depicts the resolution of earlier issues as well as the current issues of the adult stage we are now discussing.

Mayeroff discusses care in terms of its ingredients; he attempts to describe what is involved in care. The themes relevant to the first stage include those of trust and hope. Although they have the same strucure as they would at any stage, there is a different way in which they are organized around care. In caring, one trusts the other, whether the person or project, in a special way; one trusts the other to grow. Mayeroff discusses the trust involved in care in this way:

> Caring involves trusting the other to grow in its own time and in its own way. . . . The father who "cares" too much and "overprotects" his child does not trust the child, and whatever he may think he is doing, he is responding more to his own needs than to the needs of the child to grow. (1971, pp. 20-21)

Although the trust of the child leans more on the other rather than freeing the other for growth, there are still the similarities: "Trusting the other is to let go; it includes an element of risk and a leap into the unknown, both of which take courage" (p. 21). So the trust of the caring adult and of the cared-for child have a similar basic structure but, for example, the father in the above quote has the added twist of the challenge of his commitment to the well-developed ego mode of over-responsibility. Still, in responding to it with hope, the adult finds himself or herself in the same mode as anyone else in the experience of hope: "There is hope that the other will grow through my caring which is more general than hope as a specific expectation; it is akin, in some ways, to the hope that accompanies the coming of spring" (p. 25). And, again:

> Faith as a way of being, as a basic trust in life, goes with confidence in going out into the unknown in the course of realizing ourselves and caring for others. It is the antithesis of closing ourselves off through fear of the unknown; instead

178

of avoiding life, we are more
accessible to it. (p. 84)

In describing a life ordered through caring,
Mayeroff includes a "basic certainty" which, in other
terms, we had previously described as belonging to
hope. Again, although this experience is integrated
within caring, the hope that accompanies it has the
same structure as the hope of earlier stages; it is
here integrated in a new way around caring. Mayeroff
describes this basic certainty as "more like being
rooted in the world than like clinging to a rock" (p.
68) and discusses it further:

> Basic certainty requires outgrowing
> the need to feel certain, to have
> absolute guarantees as to what is or
> will be. Instead, if we think of
> basic certainty as including deep-
> seated security, it also includes
> being vulnerable and giving up the
> preoccupation with trying to be
> secure. (p. 68)

So, it is evident from these quotations that the
hope experienced by the caring adult has the same
fundamental structure as hope at any stage; yet, in
caring, the hope is organized or integrated around
the theme of the other's growth. The same is true
for the second stage issues of will. Caring involves
willing, which is the same for everyone, but it also
involves the added twist of adult promises. Mayeroff
describes this willing as follows:

> Obligations that derive from devotion
> are a constituent element in caring,
> and I do not experience them as
> forced on me or as necessary evils;
> there is a convergence between what I
> feel I am supposed to do and what I
> want to do. (p. 9)

Being autonomous, a second stage issue, also
means something different for the adult because, for
him or her, it is through caring that autonomy is re-
achieved:

> In order to live "my own life" I must
> make it my own through caring and

179

taking responsibility for it, just as
I must act on an ideal and help to
actualize it if I am to make it my
own. I am not autonomous to begin
with; autonomy is an achievement like
maturity or the growth of a significant friendship. (p. 78)

So, willing and autonomy are also integrated in
a new way under the experience of care. Imagination
is also involved in a new way in caring:

To care for another person, I must be
able to understand him and his world
as if I were inside it. . . . But
only because I understand and respond
to my own needs to grow can I
understand his striving to grow; I
can understand in another only what I
can understand in myself. (pp. 41-
42)

Mayeroff also discusses the third stage issue of
guilt, how it calls me back to the other and to
myself and how I overcome this guilt by renewed
caring even though the overcoming of guilt is not the
main motivation for my caring (p. 35). So, the call
of conscience is the same as for all the other stages
except, in this case, it is a call to adult caring.

Fourth stage issues of competence are also
integrated within the experience of caring for, as
Mayeroff indicates, "It is not enough merely to want
to care for the other and desire its growth; I must
be able to help it grow" (p. 33). Such competence
involves knowing:

To care for others, I must know many
things. I must know, for example,
who the other is, what his powers and
limitations are, what his needs are,
and what is conducive to his growth;
I must know how to respond to his
needs, and what my own powers and
limitations are. (p. 13)

And, as we discussed with regard to competence, this
knowing requires involvement:

> I cannot care by sheer habit; I must
> be able to learn from my past. I see
> what my actions amount to, whether I
> have helped or not, and, in the light
> of the results, maintain or modify my
> behavior so that I can better help
> the other. (pp. 15-16)

The competence involved in caring, as in any situation, includes the resistance of the person or project to it and appropriate disciplines with which to meet this resistance. Mayeroff discusses this in terms of the life ordered around caring:

> Such inclusive ordering requires
> giving up certain things and
> activities, and may thus be said to
> include an element of submission.
> But this submission, like the
> voluntary submission of the craftsman
> to his discipline and the
> requirements of his materials, is
> basically liberating and affirming.
> (p. 53)

In this review of life stages, as organized around caring, the fifth stage issues of identity and fidelity are also essentially involved. Mayeroff discusses identity in terms of "place":

> In the context of a man's life,
> caring has a way of ordering his
> other values and activities around
> it. When this ordering is
> comprehensive, because of the
> inclusiveness of his caring, there is
> a basic stability in his life; he is
> "in place" in the world, instead of
> being out of place, or merely
> drifting or endlessly seeking his
> place. (p. 2)

Mayeroff has more interesting things to say about the concept of place, but, for our purposes, it is enough to say that it is through caring that one finds one's adult place and one's adult identity.

The issue of constancy and devotion, which we discussed as fifth stage issues, are also integrated within caring. Mayeroff notes that devotion is essential to caring (p. 8) and he also speaks of the constancy and fidelity necessary for caring: "Caring assumes continuity, and is impossible if the other is continually being replaced. The other must remain constant, for caring is a developmental process" (p. 34). So, again, while identity and fidelity are foundational to caring, they are also integrated within it in a new way.

Caring is not merely the objective living out of obligations; it assumes as foundational also the capacity to love, which we defined as a sixth stage issue: "In the broad sense, 'being with' characterizes the process of caring itself; in caring for another person we can be said to be basically with him in his world, in contrast to simply knowing about him from outside" (p. 43). Caring also assumes that one is able to risk one's identity in becoming involved with others: "There is a selflessness in caring that is very different from the loss of self in panic or through certain kinds of conformity" (p. 29).

Caring also shares with loving the characteristic of call and response; this characteristic has been described as essential to commitment, our term for adulthood. However, we can see from the example which Mayeroff uses that the call and response structure moves more toward the issues of caring:

> I am on call for my appropriate others. . . . The man who cares for his appropriate others aspires to be always available to them when they really need him: the caring parent can be called away from something else to return to the child; the caring doctor can be reached by his patient; the caring artist is at the call of his work of art. (p. 61)

So, we can see that in caring the experiences of intimacy and love are becoming more regularized and are extended beyond the partners or the group to other people and projects.

As the virtue or strength connected with issues of the seventh stage, care shares many of the essential characteristics of earlier virtues or strengths, such as hope, will and so on. For example, as in the earlier virtues, "existence opens up in depth" (p. 74) and "Past and future . . . have an unknown and promising dimension" (p. 80). There is a movement away from fantasy: "To care for the other, I must see the other as it is and not as I would like it to be or feel it must be" (p. 19). There is a change in priorities or in what is considered to be important (p. 51). Caring is good for me and involves self-care as well (p. 48) and, finally, like the other existential modes, "Caring is compatible with a certain amount of blundering" (p. 38). There are other similarities, of course, but perhaps these are enough to make the point.

In addition to these similarities, there are also some things which are distinctive to caring:

> This, then, is the basic pattern of caring, understood as helping the other to grow: I experience the other as an extension of myself and also as independent and with the need to grow; I experience the other's development as bound up with my own sense of well-being; and I feel needed by it for that growing. I respond affirmatively and with devotion to the other's need, guided by the direction of its growth. (pp. 9-10)

Also, unlike the intimacy of the previous stage, "Caring may or may not be reciprocated" (p. 36). Mayeroff uses the examples of the young child, the patient in psychotherapy and the work of art, none of which can offer care. Caring involves gratitude not only on the part of the care-giver ("Caring becomes my way of thanking for what I have received") (p. 86) but also on the part of the recipient. One expresses gratitude by passing on the caring:

> To help another person to grow is at least to help him to care for something or someone apart from himself, and it involves encouraging and assisting him to find and create areas of his own in which he is able to care. (pp. 10-11)

Finally, caring involves self-actualization and living the meaning of my life; for us this would mean the actualization of my <u>adult</u> possibilities and the meaning of my <u>adult</u> life. In commitment, I participate in a new way in the discovery and creation of my own adult history:

> No one else can give me the meaning of my life, it is something I alone can make. The meaning is not something predetermined which simply unfolds; I help both to create it and to discover it, and this is a continuing process, not a once-and-for-all. (p. 62)

And, then, about the motivation for caring, Mayeroff adds these clarifications for a not-yet-adult age: "I do not try to help the other grow in order to actualize myself, but by helping the other grow I do actualize myself" (p. 30). Similarly, "But I do not care in order to live the meaning of my life. Instead, living a life centered around caring for my appropriate others <u>is</u> living the meaning of my life" (p. 65).

In this section we have attempted to describe the authentic experiene of caring and also to show how it integrates the strengths of previous stages in a new way. The point is made that issues are not resolved once-and-for-all at a particular stage; these issues have to be re-resolved within the context of later stages. The fear of the first stage reappears in later stages as, for example, the fear of failure or the fear of intimacy. Each step in growth involves the whole person and his or her experience. Mayeroff, in his description of caring, offers a clear demonstration of the way in which caring reawakens and reintegrates the strengths of earlier stages. Let us now proceed to a few brief descriptions of inauthentic modes surrounding the issue of care.

The Work-hound and the Conformist: Two Fallen Modes

Two ways of removing the ambiguity and the promise from the issue of care in adulthood involve reducing adult life to work (P ⟶ W) and merely going along with the external societal demands (W ⟶ P).

Rather than discovering and creating the meaning of one's adult life, the first, the work-hound, specializes in creating and lacks receptivity while the second, the conformist, specializes in discovering and lacks a sense of agency.

The work-hound develops a style in which work becomes the central and almost exclusive aspect of life. This particular mode is usually not one that springs up unexpectedly but is a continuation of an earlier fallen or fantasy mode of over-responsibility. It is this fantasy mode which is challenged by adult commitment. Unfortunately, however, the mode is socially supported and one may continue the fantasy that over-responsibility will make everything turn out all right. It may not be until the mid-life crisis that one becomes shorn of this particular illusion and this probably will be a somewhat traumatic event. The idolization of work and its rewards usually results not in satisfaction but in loneliness and alienation. The lack of receptivity and the reduction of life usually catch up with one and may lead one into the seemingly opposite mode of conformity before a crisis in the mode occurs.

In caring, as in all the authentic modes, one shapes the world and is shaped by it. The conformist becomes a specialist or an expert in being shaped. Again, such a mode is supported by society in general and it may also last untl mid-life, when it may become an issue. Van Kaam (1972) gives an example of a mode of conformity in young adulthood which he calls the mode of "public adulthood." He also discusses the social aspect of this stage.

It appears to van Kaam that mankind itself is in a period of transition from adolescence to adulthood, that we are in a kind of second adolescence with problems of its own (pp. 120-121). It is no wonder, then, that the social supports for adult caring are so weak and it also suggests that numerically there are fewer adults than is generally supposed. In the light of this social context, van Kaam describes the phenomenon of public adulthood as the conformity of the young working adult:

> To catch on to the rules of being an
> adult was not easy. It took a lot of
> energy and attention to learn how to

talk and dress properly, to please
his boss. . . . When he was an
adolescent he neglected these skills,
partly to protest against their abuse
as a false front by many. He lived
as if he were in a different
culture--a subculture. . . . Then
suddenly he was thrust into the adult
world, with a job, a family of his
own . . . he mastered as fast as he
could the way of adult society. (p.
121)

Van Kaam argues for a harmonizing of the truth
of adolescence with the truth of adulthood rather
than for a complete capitulation to the external
societal demands:

Slowly the realization dawns on him
that public adulthood is merely a
period of transition between
adolescence and genuine adulthood.
Many people get stuck in this phase.
Part of the reason may be because the
public at large seems to prefer that
people stay there. Contemporary
society tends on the whole to
identify itself with this public
stage of adult life. . . . We could
say, then, that public adulthood is
the last, perhaps the most
formidable, hindrance to be overcome
by modern man in his search for a
self-motivated life. (pp. 122-123)

The mode of public adulthood, as well as other
modes of conformity, involves a passivity
uncharacteristic of caring. Its semingly opposite
mode, that of the idolization of work, involves an
over-activity and over-responsibility just as
uncharacteristic of caring. Like the "over-caring"
father described above by Mayeroff, caring too much
is another way of not caring at all. One cannot
perfectly sustain the authentic mode of caring at all
times and a move into these fallen modes is most
common. However, according to Heidegger, it is on
the fallen modes that authentic modes are built; a
modification of these modes is what is involved in
authenticity. However, as we have seen, such modes
are not dropped easily and are apt to change only in

crisis or through disciplines.

Summary

In this chapter the second stage of adulthood has been described. Erikson's three-pronged approach under the title "generativity vs stagnation" has been broadened to include the authentic mode of adult caring. The caring mode has been shown not only to integrate the issues of generativity in a new and altered way but also to re-integrate the earlier strengths or which care itself is founded. The fallen modes of the work-hound and the conformist have been briefly described as centering on the issue of care. Let us now proceed to the last stage of development described by Erikson and sum up the broader approach suggested in this book.

CHAPTER TEN

WISDOM

In the study on commitment quoted in Chapter Six, subjects were already in some ways sounding like they were coming to the end of their commitments even though most of them were still involved in living them out. In the later moments of the commitment especially, they were already giving hints of the themes relevant to older adulthood and the final stage of development. The positive feelings they described toward the end seemed to be from the perspective of one who was older and looking back on the commitment.

There were <u>feelings of satisfaction and worth</u> expressed, a <u>feeling that it was worthwhile to do</u>, a <u>feeling that it was right and fitting</u> and, in general, <u>the falling away of negative feelings</u>. Subjects seemed to be saying that the promises they made earlier did indeed turn out to be promising in the end even though suffering, sacrifice and some unexpected turns of events occurred. As expressed in the previous chapter on caring, subjects seemed to see their adult commitments as living out the meaning of their lives. Perhaps this perspective should be kept in mind as we review this stage.

Ego Integrity vs Despair: Erikson's Three-Pronged Approach

In his description of ego integrity, Erikson (1963) seems also to emphasize the importance of adult commitments:

> Only in him who has taken care of things and people and has adapted himself to the triumphs and disappointments adherent to being, the originator of others or the generator of products and ideas--only in him may gradually ripen the fruit of these seven stages. I know no better word for it than ego integrity. (p. 268)

The ego in ego integrity for Erikson is, as we have seen, the psychoanalytic meaning of ego. In the following, he uses the terms "ego" and "self" in exactly the opposite sense in which we are using them in the model being proposed. If these terms were reversed, our meaning would come through exactly. Erikson says of ego integrity:

> It is the ego's accrued assurance of its proclivity for order and meaning. It is a post-narcissistic love of the human ego--not of the self--as an experience which conveys some world order and spiritual sense, no matter how dearly paid for. (p. 268)

For us, it would be the experience of meaning and wholeness that permeates the self, the self whose focus is the other. The ego and its role is affirmed as part of this harmonic whole, whose center is the self-world dialogue.

Erikson points out that, just as our subjects saw their commitments as right and fitting, so also does the possessor of integrity. Further, this person feels a link with his own tradition and with others:

> It is the acceptance of one's one and only life cycle as something that had to be and that, by necessity, permitted of no substitutions: it thus means a new, a different love of one's parents. It is a comradeship with the ordering ways of distant times and different pursuits. (p. 268)

In the discussion of facticity in the first chapter, it was stressed that one must live out one's own facticity, that the givens of one's life (tradition, sex, bodily inheritance, etc.) provide the boundaries within which possibility could occur. Thus, it was not possible to develop a universal personality; rather, one developed within one's own culture and, in doing so, made it possible to find links with mankind in general. Erikson seems also to be making this point:

> . . . for him [the possessor of integrity] all human integrity stands or falls with the one style of integrity of which he partakes. The

190

style of integrity developed by his
culture or civilization thus becomes
the "patrimony of his soul" . . .
Each individual, to become a mature
adult, must to a sufficient degree
develop all the ego qualities
mentioned, so that a wise Indian, a
true gentleman, and a mature peasant
share and recognize in one another
the final stage of integrity. (pp.
268-269)

However, the major point in terms of theory
which Erikson makes here is the fact that time is not
linear, that life is experienced more as a life cycle
than as a historical time line: "Webster's
Dictionary is kind enough to help us complete this
outline in a circular fashion. Trust (the first of
our ego values) is here defined as 'the assured
reliance on another's integrity,' the last of our
values" (p. 269).

We will go even further here and say that the
issue of life and death of the first stage is also
the issue for the last stage, that both the infant
and the older person are the same distance from death
or non-being and that the issue of concern is
similar. It is an issue of hope; but, just as care
integrates hope in a different way than experienced
in early life, so wisdom integrates it differently.
However, the issue of hope remains very central here,
not merely foundational. Again, this view would not
seem to be inconsistent with that of Erikson:

The lack or loss of this accrued ego
integration is signified by fear of
death: the one and only life cycle
is not accepted as the ultimate of
life. Despair expresses the feeling
that the time is now short, too short
for the attempt to start another life
and to try out alternate roads to
integrity. (pp. 268-269)

We see here the same themes of the first stage, fear
of death, despair and so on, however, this time from
the perspective of one who has lived a life and
has more or less responded to its possibilities.

So, in Erikson's description we see on the social pole the theme of the cultural ideal, on the bodily pole presumably some loss of bodily power or aptitude and on the ego pole the theme of ego integrity. We have related this stage to the experience of commitment in adulthood, to the description of the person as factical possibility and to the experience of time as lived.

The Broader Model

Erikson's three-pronged approach may again be incorporated to include the ordinary sense of ego and the aspect of the self which has been omitted in psychoanalysis and in traditional psychology in general. In broadening his approach, though, we are following his lead by using the terminology he suggests. For the ego aspect we borrow his term "renunciation"; for the self aspect, "wisdom." The broader model appears, then, as follows:

Figure 15. The eighth stage of development

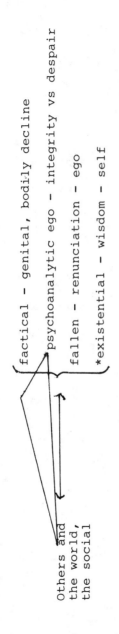

{ factical – genital, bodily decline

psychoanalytic ego – integrity vs despair

fallen – renunciation – ego

*existential – wisdom – self

Others and
the world,
the social

193

The role of the ego at this stage would seem to be renunciation of ego needs. This renunciation has, of course, been going on since infancy, and, especially in the experience of commitment, it has been accelerated. For example, in the description of caring, there is very little attention to meeting the needs of the caretaker unless the meaning of that term is stretched to include the need for meaning. However, at this stage, there seems to be a deliberate and positive renunciation which makes wisdom possible.

Concerning wisdom, it would probably be better, as with the topic of love, to be silent. We will limit ourselves to a consideration of its similarity with the first stage issue of hope, this again to emphasize the life cycle. Philosophy, of course, means the love of wisdom and Josef Pieper (1963), in a discussion of philosophy, links it with hope:

> In its fusion of positive and negative, of ignorance on the way to further knowledge, wonder reveals itself as having the same structure as hope, the same architecture as hope--the structure that characterizes philosophy and, indeed, human existence itself. We are essentially viatores, on the way, beings who are "not yet." (p. 104)

> And so the man who philosophizes and wonders is ultimately superior to one who submits to the despairing narrowness of indifference. For the former hopes! On the other hand, he is inferior to one who knows and comprehends, who finally possesses truth. Again, to wonder, to philosophize, means to hope! (p. 106)

> That which can satisfy us fully, and which we consequently desire for its own sake, is precisely what is given us in hope: "the wisdom which is sought for its own sake," Aquinas says, "is something which cannot become man's possession"; that wisdom, he goes on to say, is really

only given to man in the form of a
loan. (p. 108)

This link-up between the first stage and the last
stage   provides us a clue to the discovery of the
inauthentic modes related to this issue.

Fear and Apathy:
Two Fallen Modes

Fear, which has been described as the first
negative emotion and the foundation for all of the
fallen modes, also appears to be the fallen mode for
the last stage. However, the object of the fear is
not as disguised as in earlier stages and it is more
clearly seen as the fear of death. With the lived
certainty now that one is going to die, one faces
directly the chaos and the meaninglessness, and up
against that puts the integrity of one's life style
as lived out in one's history. As in other authentic
moments, in wisdom the past as well as the future is
experienced as open to possibility, primarily the
possibility of understanding the meaning of one's
life and the broader themes of life and death.

The same themes of fear as described in the
first stage are also present here except that one
does not have a long stretch of life ahead. As
Erikson (1963) describes the situation:

> The lack or loss of this accrued ego
> integration is signified by fear of
> death: the one and only life cycle is
> not accepted as the ultimate of life.
> Despair expresses the feeling that
> the time is now short, too short for
> the attempt to start another life and
> to try out alternate roads to
> integrity. (pp. 268-269)

Still, in the face of this situation, hope and wisdom
would still suggest the possibility of acceptance.
The living out of this possibility also has a broader
social effect:

195

> And it seems possible to further
> paraphrase the relation of adult
> integrity and infantile trust by
> saying that healthy children will not
> fear life if their elders have
> integrity enough not to fear death.
> (Erikson, 1963, p. 269)

The current social situation, the separation of older people from the rest, the emphasis on production and the lack of appreciation of true leisure are all conditions which foster fear in older people and make it difficult for them to preserve hope. This fear may also hypnotize and entrance them so that in despair they exhibit the same apathy as we observed in institutionalized infants. These two modes, fear (P $\longrightarrow$ W) and apathy (W $\longrightarrow$ P), like the other fallen modes, are actually two moments of the same mode.

An Example of Integrity:
Three Approaches

Most people would probably agree that Gandhi's life would qualify as an example of integrity, that he came closer to an experience of true adulthood than most others. Let us consider three approaches to an understanding of Gandhi's life in order to emphasize the importance of one's theoretical perspective. The theoretical position one takes does determine the limits of what one sees and understands and how one understands it.

The point has often been made throughout this volume that traditional psychology omits the self mode, the existential mode as described, for example, by the titles of these chapters. Because of this lack, the self mode has to be reduced to what is familiar and that is the ego mode. In terms of the theory presented here, in traditional psychology, hope becomes reduced to prediction, will to control, imagination to planning, competence to technique, fidelity to constancy, love to affiliation, care to production and wisdom to renunciation. This is a definite bias in traditional psychology and it narrows greatly the limits of understanding.

Even when one attempts to be humanistic and even phenomenological in approach, the lack of a theoretical justification for a self leads to a very impoverished understanding. The text <u>Perceptual Psychology</u> (Combs, Richards and Richards, 1976) provides an example of how Gandhi is understood in traditional psycyology. This example is all the more telling since it is not one of the more typical objectivistic approaches of traditional psychology; in fact, its subtitle indicates that it is a humanistic approach to the study of persons. We may rightly assume that the more typical approaches would be and are more extreme in reducing the self to the ego. In fact, many behavioral approaches would not only deny that there is a self but even that there is an ego or a subject at all.

Combs, Richards and Richards (1976) mention Gandhi in a section dealing with techniques for accomplishing mastery over people. The technical attitude so often mentioned in this text is very evident here. Value-oriented behavior is reduced to a matter of technique. In the introduction to the section we read:

> The techniques people use to achieve the satisfaction of need are almost as individual as the persons themselves. Some are essentially defensive, motivated by feelings of inadequacy and designed to maintain a threatened self. Others are expressions of more positive feelings of adequacy and are directed more to enhancement rather than defense of self. (p. 144)

Gandhi's techniques, rather than being in the service of India, are apparently of the latter kind, for the enhancement of himself.

The section on mastery over people, in which Gandhi is included, begins by talking about the use of force, such as beating people with a club. It continues:

> The clenched fist is still a favorite technique for achieving fundamental goals. The fist may be disguised as legal action, social position, employer-employee relationship, or presumed superiority of knowledge as

197

in a teacher-pupil relationship, but
the principle is the same. (p. 145)

Another example given is the technique of using
ordinary polite conversation to build up one's self-
concept by dominating the listener (p. 146).

However, Gandhi's techniques are included in a
subsection entitled "demonstrations of superiority,"
in which kidding, ribbing, hazing, practical joking,
ostentatious spending and giving of gifts are put
forth as examples (p. 146). Then, the specific
reference to Gandhi:

> Another interesting variation of the
> use of subtle aggression is often
> seen in clinical experience with a
> negative or dawdling child. This is
> a form of indirect aggression put to
> effective use on a larger scale by
> Gandhi and his followers in India
> and in our own country by labor in
> strikes and slowdowns in industrial
> disputes. The civil rights movement
> successfully used sit-ins and
> boycotts to protest discrimination
> and injustice. In all of these cases
> the technique is useful to gain a
> feeling of power over those who would
> force one action or another on a
> person or a group. (pp. 146-147)

The approach taken in this book is to affirm the
truth of perspectives as perspectives. If one adopts
the technical approach in attempting to understand
Gandhi, then a certain truth can be revealed. But
the narrow perspective becomes totalized and
misunderstanding rather than understanding results;
Gandhi becomes perceived primarily as a manipulator.
The technical perspective needs to be integrated into
a broader framework in which there is a place for the
authentic self and its modes. Obviously, the above
description of Gandhi is inadequate for a human
psychology.

The approach given above is somewhat reminiscent
of the early studies of famous figures in which these
figures were reduced to the narrow perspective of
psychoanalysis. The study of President Wilson (Freud
and Bullitt, 1966) is probably most representative of

this approach. Fortuntely, however, this practice has been discontinued; the neo-psychoanalytic thinkers, especially, have opened up the perspective of psychoanalysis.

Karen Horney (1950), for example, puts forth a concept of the real self (p. 17) which seems to have much in common with the self mode presented in this book. It should be clear, though, that in doing so, she is moving beyond the traditional psychoanalytic perspective which has no place for a theoretical construct like the real self. One suspects that her experience led her to violate the theoretical perspective in this way.

The second approach to understanding Gandhi to be mentioned here is also in the neo-psychoanalytic orientation and it also reflects a moving beyond the traditional psychoanalytic perspective. In Gandhi's Truth (1969) Erikson repeats what he has done in his developmental theory. He shows the way in which the biological past, the social setting and the ego development of Gandhi are intertwined and, as usual, very penetrating insights are achieved. When he discusses the ego crises of identity, intimacy and generativity with regard to Gandhi, he again expands the ego pole to touch on the realm of value and spirit. However, as in the developmental theory he hints at the self mode but doesn't develop it and the concept of ego, initiated in psychoanalysis, is just too narrow to support the experiences of the self mode. Erikson again leaves us appreciative of his contributions and frustrated at his insistence on remaining within a psychoanalytic paradigm which, even though broadened, omits a major portion of human eperience.

The third approach, of course, is the integrative approach suggested in this text. It would accept the point made by Combs, Richards and Richards (1976, pp. 146-147) that Gandhi was clever and that he used his intelligence; however, it would be stressed that this was in the service of values. It would also accept most gratefully the points made by Erikson concerning the intertwining of the past with the social opportunities and ego crises. However, in order to understand Gandhi and especially his integrity and wisdom, it would be necessary to pick up on Erikson's leads and proceed to an understanding of the value commitments of Gandhi's deepest self. And this brings us to one final observation.

From Dasein to Being

Heidegger's term for the human existent was Dasein and he defined Dasein as openness to Being. In Being and Time (1927/1962) he started by describing Dasein's side of this relationship, which we might call the subject pole of the dialogue. Later on he moved to a concentration on Being, that to which the Dasein is open. Perhaps this gives us some indication of the direction we also should take.

What does it mean to live in a psychological age? Although we may congratulate ourselves on an apparently more humane and civilized approach as represented by the psychological age, it also seems to be true that something is amiss. It is often said that people concentrate on themselves and their psychology when they have missed their mission in life, when they are confused. It seems to be no easy achievement to move beyond the ego to the world and others. However, as we have seen, the richest experiences of human life are not those of ego preoccupation but are those which involve commitment to someone or something other than ourselves. This brings us into the realm of freedom, of values and of projects that make a difference to others. Perhaps we have exhausted the themes of psychological preoccupation and may now move on to adulthood.

REFERENCES

Adler, A. (1929). The science of living. Garden City, New York: Garden City Publishing Co.

Adler, A. (1964). Advantages and disadvantages of the inferiority feeling. In H.L. Ansbacher & R.R. Ansbacher (Eds.), Superiority and social interest (pp. 50-58). Evanston, Illinois: Northwestern University Press. (Original work published 1933).

Allport, G.W. (1962). Psychological models for guidance. Harvard Educational Review, 32, 373-381.

Arieti, S. (1972). The will to be human. New York: Dell.

Assagioli, R., & Miller, S. (1972). The will of Roberto Assagioli. Intellectual Digest, 90-92.

Becker, E. (1973). The denial of death. New York: Free Press.

Bettelheim, B. (1959). Joey: A "mechanical boy." Reprinted from Scientific American.

Bettelheim, B. (1977). The uses of enchantment. New York: Vintage Books.

Binswanger, L. (1963). Heidegger's analytic of existence and its meaning for psychiatry. In J. Needleman (Trans.), Being in the World (pp. 206-221). New York: Harper and Row.

Bowlby, J. (1952). Maternal care and mental health. Geneva: World Health Organization.

Combs, A.W., Richards, A.C., & Richards, F. (1976). Perceptual psychology. New York: Harper & Row.

Cummings, N.A. (1979). Turning bread into stones: Our modern antimiracle. American Psychologist, 34, 1119-1129.

Erikson, E.H. (1961). The roots of virtue. In J. Huxley (Ed.), The humanist frame (pp. 147-165). New York: Harper and Brothers.

Erikson, E.H. (1963). Childhood and society. New York: W.W. Norton.

Erikson, E.H. (1968). Identity: Youth and crisis. New York: W.W. Norton.

Erikson, E.H. (1969). Gandhi's truth. New York: W.W. Norton.

Farley, E. (1975). Psychopathology and human evil. Lectures presented at Duquesne University, Pittsburgh, Pa., October.

Frankl, V.E. (1969). The will to meaning. New York: New American Library.

Frankl, V.E. (1971). The doctor and the soul (R. Winston & C. Winston, Trans.) (rev. ed.). New York: Bantam Books. (Original work published 1946).

Freud, S., & Bullitt, W.C. (1966). Thomas Woodrow Wilson. Boston: Houghton Mifflin.

Freud, S. (1971). Character and anal eroticism. In S.R. Maddi (Ed.), Perspectives on personality (pp. 39-43). Boston: Little, Brown. (Original work published 1908).

Gelven, M. (1970). A commentary on Heidegger's "Being and time". New York: Harper & Row.

Giorgi, A. (1970). Psychology as a human science. New York: Harper & Row.

Götz, I.L. (1974). Loneliness. Humanitas, 10, 289-299.

Gratton, M.C. (1975). A theoretical-empirical study of the lived experience of interpersonal trust. Unpublished doctoral dissertation, Duquesne University, Pittsburgh.

Gross, D., & Bloch, E. (1972). The dialectics of hope. In D. Howard & K. Klare (Eds.), The unknown dimension: European marxism since Lenin. New York: Basic Books.

Heidegger, M. (1962). *Being and time*. (J. Macquarrie & E. Robinson, Trans.). New York: Harper & Row. (Original work published 1927).

Herrigel, E. (1971). *Zen in the art of archery*. (R.F.C. Hull, Trans.). New York: Random. (Original work published 1953).

Horney, K. (1950). *Neurosis and human growth*. New York: W.W. Norton.

Jager, B. (1971). Horizontality and verticality: A phenomenological exploration into lived space. In A. Giorgi, W.F. Fischer, & R. Von Eckartsberg (Eds.), *Duquesne studies in phenomenological psychology: Volume I* (pp. 212 235). Pittsburgh: Duquesne University Press.

Jourard, S.M. (1972). Some notes on the experience of commitment. *Humanitas, 8*, 5-8.

Kilpatrick, W. (1975). *Identity and intimacy*. New York: Dell.

Laing, R.D. (1965). *The divided self*. Baltimore: Penguin Books.

Lowe, G.R. (1972). *The growth of personality*. Baltimore: Penguin Books.

Marcel, G. (1962). *Homo viator: Introduction to a metaphysic of hope* (E. Craufurd, Trans.). New York: Harper & Row. (Original work published 1951).

Marcel, G. (1964). *Creative fidelity* (R. Rosthal, Trans.). New York: Farrar, Straus.

May, R. (1969). *Love and will*. New York: Dell.

Mayeroff, M. (1971). *On caring*. New York: Harper & Row.

Minkowski, E. (1958). Findings in a case of schizophrenic depression. In R. May, E. Angel, & H.F. Ellenberger (Eds.), *Existence* (pp. 127-138). New York: Basic Books. (Original work published 1923).

Noyes, A.P., & Kolb, L.C. (1958). Modern clinical psychiatry (5th ed.). Philadelphia: W.B. Saunders.

Pieper, J. (1963). Leisure: The basis of culture. (A. Dru, Trans.). New York: New American Library.

Pirsig, R.M. (1974). Zen and the art of motorcycle maintenance. New York: Bantam Books.

Sadler, W.A. Jr. (1974). On the verge of a lonely life. Humanitas, 10, 255 276.

Shapiro, D. (1965). Neurotic styles. New York: Basic Books.

Spitz, R. (1945). Hospitalism. The Psychoanalytic Study of the Child, 1, 53 74.

Solzhenitsyn, A.I. (1974). Letter to the Soviet leaders (H. Sternberg, Trans.). New York: Harper & Row.

van den Berg, J.H. (1966). The psychology of the sickbed. Pittsburgh: Duquesne University Press.

van Kaam, A. (1966). The art of existential counseling. Wilkes-Barre, Pennsylvania: Dimension Books.

van Kaam, A. (1972). Envy and originality. New York: Doubleday.

van Kaam, A. (1981). Explanatory charts of the science of foundational formation. Studies in Formative Spirituality, 2, 132.

von Gebsattel, V.E. (1958). The world of the compulsive. In R. May, E. Angel, & H.F. Ellenberger (Eds.), Existence (pp. 170 187). New York: Basic Books. (Original work published 1938).

Westley, R.J. (1972). The will to promise. Humanitas, 8, 9-20.

ABOUT THE AUTHOR

Richard T. Knowles, Ph.D. is currently Chairman of the Psychology Department at Duquesne University. A member of the Department since 1973, he has taught in the counseling-clinical and developmental areas in addition to maintaining a private practice in psychotherapy. In the eight years prior to 1973, he was an assistant and then associate professor in counselor education at the University of Michigan. He also served as chairman of the psychology section of a national-international project on moral education. The results of this work are presented in another publication of UPA entitled <u>Psychological foundations of moral education</u>, a volume which he coedited.